Free to
Be Me

Free to Be Me

Guided Journaling
for Personal
and Spiritual Growth

Patricia Johnson-Laster

Free to Be Me: Guided Journaling for Personal and Spiritual Growth
Copyright © 2014 by Patricia Johnson-Laster, Ed.D.
Published by Deep River Books
Sisters, Oregon
www.deepriverbooks.com

ISBN-13: 9781940269054
ISBN-10: 1940269059

Library of Congress: 2013958116

Printed in the USA
2014—First Edition
22 21 20 19 18 17 16 15 14 13   10 9 8 7 6 5 4 3 2 1

Cover design by Robin Black, www.InspirioDesign.com

Contents

Introduction

Personal and spiritual growth are lifetime processes: vibrant, exhilarating, demanding, and fun. They also include painful moments of self-examination and stretching, expecially for those who bring unresolved childhood issues into the process.

As a college professor of psychology, I spent more time talking individually with students about their unsettled questions than I spent teaching in the classroom. While not necessarily experiencing a diagnosed psychological disorder, the attempts made by these young adults to live the Christian life were frequently hindered by their struggles with issues from their early family life. Like my students, I also faced unresolved issues growing up; and, although my training in psychology was valuable in helping me find answers, it was through God's words and the devotional times that I spent with Him that I was able to break free from the emotional baggage I carried with me. This, my reader, is what I want to share with you. Perhaps you will find, as I did, that when you lean on Him, every circumstance, no matter how difficult, and every situation, no matter how painful, provide opportunities. Through them, you can grow. With His guidance, they can be a vehicle for you to reach even higher places of personal and spiritual fulfillment.

This workbook provides guided journaling to help you resolve issues left from your childhood, to grow spiritually, and to gain confidence. Each of the ten steps includes four to six exercises, and each exercise is made up of three components: "Spiritual prep" time (Scripture study), journaling, and related activities. Case histories are derived from my work with students and colleagues as well as from my own personal experiences. All names have been changed. It is my hope that, after reading the brief reflection on each topic, the reader will begin his or her own journey toward personal and spiritual fulfillment by responding fully (and in writing) to the questions, engaging in the activities suggested, and completing the Scripture readings provided.

Although the workbook allows the reader to proceed at his or her own pace, it is suggested that at least one day or more be given to work through each exercise. This would provide optimal opportunity to deal with and move beyond the issues covered in a particular exercise.

Reading, journaling, and Scripture study may be done in either a group or private setting. For more details on how to do this in a group setting, see the appendix, "Leading a 'Free to Be Me' Small Group." If you choose to do this in a small-group setting, remember that group members' responses are always voluntary, and be sure that everyone honors the confidentiality of the group setting.

Remember, you are not alone. You can discover the unique, creative self that God intended you to be! God will lift you out of the ashes and weave your brokenness into a strong, durable fabric of singular beauty. Someday you will know the happiness of a Son-soaked spirit and may even be surprised to find yourself leaping with joy as you relinquish your tightly clutched baggage to Him. You, too, will know the freedom of a being a whole, healthy person created in His image.

And you will know the truth, and the truth will make you free.
John 8:32, NASB

Section One

Ashes
on
Fertile
Ground

When Only Ashes Are Left

Exercise 1

. . . .

OUT FROM BEHIND THE MASK

The LORD does not look at the things people look at. People look
at the outward appearance, but the LORD looks at the heart.
1 Samuel 16:7

O n a bright morning, as the sun gentled the edges of a cold winter day, I settled into an overstuffed recliner with a mug of hot tea and my well-worn Bible. In the quietness of the early morning, my thoughts began to wander over my years spent teaching and counseling in a small, church-related college. I remembered Anna.

Anna approached my desk one day after a class discussion on parenting and asked if she could talk with me. That session turned into many as she revealed her story.

Anna was an unwanted child. Her parents took care of her physical needs but pretty much ignored Anna—except when they reminded her how ugly she was, how stupid, or how much she lacked personality. Anna grew up believing her parents' comments and that no one could ever possibly like her if they knew what she was really like. A very intelligent person, she quickly tuned in to what others wanted from her and tried to be whatever the person wanted. But it wasn't her; it was a mask. And the real Anna, fighting for survival, would surface eventually, only to alienate her friends with her deception.

Through her college years as Anna and I continued to talk and pray together, she made great strides. I was delighted when God brought a kind and patient young man into Anna's life who understood the scars left from her background. They are now happily married with a son of their own. More and more, Anna is able to put away the various masks she is tempted to wear and allow God to use her authentic self in His service.

Anna trusts God's love for her and, in that love, has grown to value the person she really is. She is becoming a whole, confident, and consistent person. She knows it will continue to be a daily effort to master the lifelong task of being consistent in thoughts and actions. But as Anna and I both agreed years ago, the point is to try, to keep on trying, and to never give up the effort.

Thank goodness God can see beyond outward appearances! To be a person who is whole and consistent in motive and appearance may be one of the most difficult tasks we encounter on our pilgrimage. It's a risky thing to be true to who we are. It involves working through and then putting aside past hurts, misunderstandings, and betrayals. It involves relinquishing the external protective shield that we use as our mask. It demands risk and vulnerability and a mind centered on Christ. But if you make the effort, God will walk with you each step of the way—and He will never, never let go of your hand.

May God be with you as you, too, make the effort to reach a place of wholeness and consistency in your life.

SPIRITUAL PREP: Psalms 51:6; John 7:24; 2 Corinthians 4:16; Ephesians 3:14–19; 1 Thessalonians 5:23–24

Getting to Know Myself as a Child of God

My full name:

My nickname:

The day and year I was born:

Where I went to school:

My favorite subjects in school:

This is the way other people know me:

This is the secret self that I don't let others see:

Living as a Child of God

Find a photograph of yourself as a child and tape or glue it to the inside of the front cover of this workbook. That child is still a part of you. Each day, take a few minutes to study the photograph and say a prayer to God for that child. Allow Him to show you how much He loves the child in the photograph. Absorb that love. Continue this exercise throughout your use of this book.

PRAYER: Lord, help me to become a person of compassion and Christ-like selflessness
in both my inner heart and outward appearance. Help me to deal with, and then forget, past wrongs
in order to become the authentic Christ-in-me person You created me to be.

Exercise 2

• • • • • • • • • • • • • • • •

MOVING BEYOND FAILURE

*But whatever were gains to me I now consider loss for the sake of Christ. What is
more, I consider everything a loss because of the surpassing
worth of knowing Christ Jesus my Lord.*
Philippians 3:7–8

Matt had the small group laughing as he described how he gathered a bunch of daisies for a friend, Emily, and placed them on the front seat of her car. "What a nice surprise they'll be," he thought. The only problem was that it was a miserably hot summer day; and, with the sun beating down on the car, the flowers wilted. All Emily found was a terribly dreary bunch of stems and shriveled daisy petals. "We had a good laugh over those wilted flowers, but they reminded me of something," Matt said as his mood turned serious. "No matter how hard I work, it just seems that any critical remark from a friend, any misunderstanding, any mistake makes me feel like my life is only a dreary bunch of dried-up weeds and shriveled petals. Sometimes I just want to give up."

Matt's parents divorced when Matt was only a toddler, and after the divorce Matt's mom became depressed, bitter, and resentful of having to raise a child alone. For a long time, Matt thought that it was his fault that his dad had left, especially since his father didn't want any more to do with them once he was gone. Matt remembers feeling left alone a lot or being punished by his mom, but he has trouble recalling any time that he was praised or encouraged. Later, when Matt was chatting with me in my office, I asked him to explain his comments about the shriveled flowers. "Well," he said, "I try too hard to please others and I know it, but I just can't seem to stop and I'm so tired." Matt's insecurity and desperate need for love and acceptance drove him to higher and higher self-expectations. He repeatedly felt caught in his own trap of working to gain respect and approval. Matt explained that he knew he could only achieve a sense of worth by God's love and grace; however, he felt so undeserving of it, so hopeless about changing his tendency to try and please others that God seemed too distant to help. Actually, he admitted, he frequently felt that God disapproved of him also.

As I watched God's patience and persistent love forge its way deeper into Matt's heart over the next few years, I was amazed at what a confident, tranquil person he eventually became. One day, as graduation and his wedding date to Emily drew near, Matt talked to me about what had led to his change. He told me that God had finally made him realize that his self-worth rested completely in God's love for him, no matter what others thought. Through Christian friends, teachers, and counselors whom God brought into his life, Matt gradually began to see why he was so driven to win the approval of others. Deprived of the support and encouragement that he needed as a child, he continued to serve the master of unmet needs. Only when he started to understand that God knew and cared about his past and the pain that he carried was he able to loosen his grasp and let God start to heal his heart with His perfect love and acceptance. As Matt's daily walk with Him deepened, he began to understand that God, alone, was adequate to meet his deepest needs.

Let me point out that it is certainly not unhealthy to cherish acceptance, recognition, respect, and affection from others. I believe that God reinforces how much He loves us by bringing individuals into our lives who care for and accept us. Yet, while we appreciate and enjoy the attention of others, the driving force of an authentic Christian's life is God's love. As Matt discovered, nothing surpasses the awareness of His love and the joy of His presence as we walk daily with Him.

Spiritual Prep: Proverbs 3:21–26; 14:26, Isaiah 30:15a; John 14:12; Hebrews 4:16

Getting to Know Myself as a Child of God

Describe your father:

Describe your mother:

Living as a Child of God

The person who has loved me most in my life:

What I would like to say to this person:

PRAYER: Lord Jesus, show me my worth and value in Your eyes.

Exercise 3

. . . .

DEALING WITH LIMITATIONS

*For all those who exalt themselves will be humbled, and those
who humble themselves will be exalted.*
Luke 14:11

Frankie is a knockout! She has fine auburn hair, porcelain skin, large green eyes, and a lovely figure without even working at it. Growing up, we were more like sisters than best friends. But, alas, we looked nothing alike. When we reached adolescence, Frankie entered and won several beauty contests—and she deserved to win! She had a personality as lovely as her physical appearance, and I was always delighted to hear of her victories.

This story, however, is not about Frankie, but about those of us who are not as fortunate as her. Most of us are considerably less than perfect. There's a flaw or two in our physical appearance. We may lack some of the charming personality traits which make some people so popular. And, perhaps, we're not among those in the upper percentile of every intelligence test. It's not too difficult to become enmeshed in our limitations. We can fall into the trap, almost like reclining on a soft cushion of self-pity, of giving up and dwelling on our shortcomings.

If hopelessness and self-doubt start to dominate our thoughts, we can also feel like we're not capable of serving God in any way. We think He doesn't want our pathetic lives used in service to Him. Instead we waste time ruminating over our fate: how unfair life has been to us and how badly we are treated, how insignificant and ignored we are, and how dismal the future seems to us. I know! I've found myself in that place many times. How easy it is to forget Jesus' admonition, "Do not let your hearts be troubled" (John 14:1).

What if, instead of fretting over our limitations and those qualities we lack, we face these limitations courageously? What if, instead of insisting that God make us perfect, we willingly lay our flawed selves on the altar of sweet sacrifice to God to be used by Him—flaws, warts, and all? Perhaps humility means that we stop demanding to be super-persons before making ourselves available to others and to Him. I believe God knows how much courage it takes to risk exposure of our weaknesses to the world. I believe He especially delights in us when we do so, trusting Him and realizing that our successes will be attributed to His strength rather than to our own talents. It doesn't matter that we're not the most attractive nor intelligent people alive. It doesn't matter that we lack natural charm and grace. It doesn't matter that we're imperfect, nor that we've failed repeatedly. He has a plan for each of us. Our hope and our value rest on our willingness to trust Him with our circumstances and to let Him use us in the fulfillment of His creative, exciting plan for our lives.

SPIRITUAL PREP: Matthew 25:14-30

Getting to Know Myself as a Child of God

What is my best personality trait?

What is my least favorite personality trait?

What are my limitations as I see them?

Who would I most like to resemble, and why?

Living as a Child of God

Spend a few quiet moments asking God to show you how He can use your personality traits. Write down ways that you think He will use you in His service:

PRAYER: Father God, I surrender to You my weaknesses, my limitations, my shortcomings.
I ask You to use them to Your glory. Make my attitude a positive one, and make me eager to share
Your love with others who need to know You.

Exercise 4

· · · · · · · · · · · · · · · · ·

SETTING NEW PRIORITIES

Jesus replied: "'Love the Lord your God with all your heart and with all your soul and with all your mind.'
This is the first and greatest commandment. And the second is like it: 'Love your neighbor as yourself.'"
Matthew 22:37–39

Getting our priorities in order is not an easy task, but it is a very important one. In the above Scripture passage, a picture is drawn of the priority that loved ones should take in our lives. Getting that picture into focus is more difficult if we believe ourselves unlovely, worthless, an object of scorn. It troubles me that many folks teach that humility means self-devaluation. If we accept this definition, we might, in a misguided attempt to be humble, avoid looking at our positive qualities and focus only on how inferior we believe ourselves to be to others. Matthew 22:37–39 clearly shows how God expects us to prioritize ourselves in the scheme of things. There is no hierarchy between us and others. In fact, there's a secret for loving others. If we can forgive and love ourselves, even as Christ forgives and loves us, than it is so much easier to really love others! So, go ahead, allow God to show you how to love yourself and see how much easier it is for you to love your spouse, your parent, your friend, and your neighbor.

In these verses, I think God is telling us to love others and I think He's also gently reminding us that we need to love ourselves. Both love of self and love of others, however, are to be subordinate to love for God. No one—child, parent, husband, wife, friend—can share the position God occupies in our affections. While we are never instructed to belittle ourselves, we are instructed to love God first and to place all our earthly possessions in His hands.

Impossible though it may seem and excruciatingly painful though it may be, we must be willing to release our love for others to God before our hearts can completely know the fullness of the Christ living within us. Then glory! The truth becomes clear! Christ loves us, as well as those dear folks we cherish, even more than we dreamed it possible to love. But for us to cling to others out of our own need might destroy them in its demanding, possessive grasp. To make others the source of our lives leaves us disillusioned and bitter when they fail to live up to expectations that no person can meet. To look to them for life's answers leads us to despair, and we often carry grudges when they fail us.

To love others as Christ loves them, to put God first and to let Him love others through us: that is to know the authentic, affirming, unfathomable meaning of love. In giving up, we gain. In releasing, we attain. We walk as new creatures, with Christ as the focus of our lives and love for our dear ones as an outpouring of His presence in our hearts.

SPIRITUAL PREP: Deuteronomy 6:4–5; Matthew 10:37–39; Mark 12:29–31; 1 John 5:2–3

Getting to Know Myself as a Child of God

My top three priorities are:

My next ten priorities are

Living as a Child of God

Look over the lists of priorities you just made. Spend a few minutes in prayer asking God if there are any changes in your priorities you feel He's leading you to make. Rewrite your priorities according to those changes:

PRAYER: Lord Jesus, help me to love myself and others as You love me;
but, most of all, help me to love You supremely.

Exercise 5

. . . .

MAKING THE PILGRIMAGE

*You have searched me, LORD, and you know me. You know when I sit and
when I rise; you perceive my thoughts from afar.*
Psalm 139:1–2

Jennifer had a beautiful testimony, and she shared it with me one Friday afternoon when her classes were finished for the week. As she told her story, Jennifer expressed how much her parents loved her and wondered why she had made so many destructive choices. Jennifer's parents were lax and undemanding in their approach to parenting. They were so involved in their own problems that they had little energy for child-rearing. They made few demands of Jennifer and rarely exerted any contol over her behavior. Jennifer was allowed to act on her impulses without either positive or negative consequences. She was given no boundaries and received no discipline.

Jennifer possessed keen intelligence but performed poorly in school. She was impulsive and generally not liked by her peers. Desperate to gain friends, Jennifer made self-destructive choices involving drugs, promiscuity, and attempts at suicide. There seemed to be no depth to which she wouldn't sink—until she met Alex. Alex was a strong Christian who took an interest in Jennifer and invited her to his church. Grateful for his friendship, Jennifer began to attend and participate in the youth group at Alex's church. There, she accepted Christ into her life.

Still, Jennifer told me, she would continue to falter and make bad choices. Yet God never gave up on her. Jennifer said that God let her know over and over that no matter what she did, He was with her. God was always ready to forgive her and help her grow. As He made Jennifer more and more aware of His love through her prayerful study of His word, she gradually began developing new goals and exercising more self-control. She pulled her grades up and formed healthier relationships. In doing so, Jennifer began to regard herself as a person with dignity and value. By the time I had met her, Jennifer was able to hold her head high and her shoulders back and face the world with confidence. God had taught her this.

This search for self is one we all must travel, but it is an individual pilgrimage. If you are about to embark on this journey, here are some things that might help you:

- Turn to God daily in private prayer and Scripture study as you read this book.
- Under His guidance, set goals for your life.
- Prayerfully establish boundaries for what you will and will not do.
- Seek out resources you need—books, counselors, leaders in your church—to help you sustain the boundaries you set and reach your goals.

If you faithfully set aside time each day to spend talking with and listening to God, to reading His word, light will be shed on your search for self-identity. No one can make this pilgrimage for you, but never doubt that it's an honorable one. God wants you to know yourself. An unexamined, shallow sense of identity accounts for much of the unhappiness and superficiality found in the lives of many Christians. Don't give up. God wants you to accept and assume responsibility for yourself. He wants you to love yourself as He loves you. As you learn to accept and love yourself, you'll find that you're also increasingly free to accept and love others.

SPIRITUAL PREP: 2 Samuel 22: 29–31; Psalm 19:12–14; Proverbs 14:8; Jeremiah 9:23–24; I Corinthians 2:9–12

Getting to Know Myself as a Child of God

My goals as a child:

Have your goals changed since childhood? If so, write out your goals as they now are:

Living as a Child of God

Spend some time in prayer asking God to show you boundaries that you need to set for your life. Make two lists below:

1. Unacceptable activities that are outside the boundaries for the life I choose to live.

2. Activities I enjoy doing that are within the boundaries I set for my life.

Reminder: Are you continuing the special exercise you began in the first step of this chapter? Did you find a photograph of yourself as a child and attach it to the inside front cover of this workbook where you can see it each day? Continue, when you see the photograph of yourself as a child, to pause, pray, and absorb the love which God had and has for you as His child.

PRAYER: Father, I open my heart and life to You. Please heal the broken pieces from the past and fill those needs that were never met. Convince my doubting heart that in Your eyes I am altogether lovely.

The Ashes of Self-Defeating Attitudes

Exercise 1

. . . .

DISCOURAGEMENT

The eternal God is your refuge, and underneath are the everlasting arms.
Deuteronomy 33:27

I'm bored and I don't feel like there's anything I can do to make life better," Brad said as we began our first counseling session. Brad was not a traditional student. He had worked for many years at a variety of jobs, mostly common labor. He felt that all those years had been terribly wasted. Now he was older than most students and ashamed that he had waited so long to try and make something of his life. Even though the minister of his church had encouraged him to take courses at our college, Brad was uncertain that he could succeed in academic work. I was truly happy that Brad had started taking classes. Still, I remember feeling saddened that he allowed himself to become defeated by self-doubt and discouragement, not recognizing how intelligent and talented he was and how much he had to offer. It took Brad three years of college to begin to develop enduring confidence, but during that time he became a friend and a caring model to many of the younger students who looked up to him. Brad, along with his sweet family, is now serving as a missionary on a foreign mission field.

Every life has periods of discouragement. It is during these interminably long stretches that the tasks we've been given to do may seem trivial. When there's no recognition for our efforts, when no one seems to be profoundly touched or changed by coming into contact with us, we begin to question, "What value am I, Lord?" We want to hold great revivals, win souls, build new churches, and not feel as if life is passing us by while we wallow in the doldrums. Those whose early years taught them to doubt themselves and their abilities are especially vulnerable to feelings of discouragement and boredom; they may give up entirely if they don't see immediate results in their attempts to live Christ-like lives.

Although life may seem barren and unproductive, God will often take the times of "everydayness" and fill them with opportunities for us to use the special abilities He has given each of us. It is possible to overcome our reluctance to exercise those abilities if we put our trust in Him to use our efforts and bring about the plan He has for our lives. During the long stretches of everydayness, the greatest work is often accomplished by those who walk most humbly, most quietly with Him.

Our lives can become rivers of living water to persons in our paths at school, in the neighborhood, at the office, or sitting next to us on an airplane. If, in the still moments, our goal is to draw closer to God, He will honor this goal, bind us more tightly in His arms of love, and put a song in our hearts. He will use the abilities He's given us—even in quiet, uneventful times—if we strive to remain close to His heart.

SPIRITUAL PREP: Psalms 37:7; Isaiah 25:9; 40:31; Hebrews 10:36; James 1:4

Getting to Know Myself as a Child of God

Was there a pattern of discouragement in your childhood? Describe any discouragement you felt below. Include phrases, facial expressions, and mannerisms used by those who discouraged you:

How did you deal with the discouragement?

Living as a Child of God

This is an important step for you to take: Think quietly for a few minutes about what you'd like to tell those who discouraged you as a child. Write what you'd like to say to them now:

PRAYER: Lord Jesus, when all seems trivial and unproductive,
put Your song in my heart and overflow my life with rivers of Your love.

Exercise 2

· · · · · · · · · · · · · · · ·

FRUSTRATION

When morning came, there was Leah! So Jacob said to Laban, "What is this you
have done to me? I served you for Rachel, didn't I? Why have you deceived me?"
Genesis 29:25

My car refused to start. There it sat, several thousand pounds of useless steel, leaving me with no means of getting to my appointments that day. Grudgingly, I walked to the campus where I taught and, once there, I requested keys to the school's car to reach an urgent dental appointment later that day.

As the afternoon wore on, I caught myself trapped in my office listening to a small group of students who were adamantly expressing their dislike of a fellow faculty member. Minutes crept close to my appointment time. I rushed out of my office at the last minute to get to the college car, only to find that the keys were not where they were supposed to be.

Frantically, I searched for the person responsible for the car. Unable to find him, I telephoned the dentist's office to delay my appointment but was unable to hear the extremely soft voice at the other end of the line.

I felt totally frustrated. I was disappointed by the person who misplaced the keys. I was upset with the students for taking my time to complain about another teacher. I was upset at the administration for paying a salary too inadequate to repair the car sitting in my driveway at home. I became angry at the person with the soft voice on the other end of the telephone line for failing to speak louder. I had become absorbed with all the minor irritations that had amassed within a few short minutes and was blaming everyone and everything for my frustration. Where was all the joy and gentle love with which my heart had been blessed that very morning as I had spent time with God?

When life seems to crash around us and everything goes wrong, we need to pause, catch our breath, and challenge any blaming or aggressive response we have to the situation. It's true, a loved one may have let us down, fellowship with a Christian friend might have been broken because of misunderstanding, our promotion at work might be overlooked. We might be the victim rather than the recipient of favoritism. Rather than letting our whole outlook become clouded and darkened by events, a more effective coping strategy would be to take the matter to God and anticipate His guidance in assessing and dealing with it. He may answer us through words of Scripture; He may shed light on our situation by leading us to talk to a Christian friend; He might respond with the gentle nudging of His Holy Spirit. We can always count on Him to grant us His wisdom.

Review today's Scripture passage again. Frustration will pass. Leah was eventually blessed with more children than Rachel. Jacob served Laban for another seven years and went on to become one of the great patriarchs. Perhaps their victory was won because their eyes were focused more on the sovereign God than on the temporary thorns in their pathways.

SPIRITUAL PREP: Romans 5:3–5; Colossians 1:11–12; 2 Thessalonians 1:4; Hebrews 12:1–2; James 5:7–11

Getting to Know Myself as a Child of God

Describe three things, no matter how minor, that really frustrate you:

How do you respond to each of these frustrations?

Living as a Child of God

Take a few moments and reflect on what you just wrote. Is there a way that you'd rather deal with frustration than how you described above? Spend a few minutes in prayer, asking for God's wisdom and guidance and listening for His response. Describe how the Lord might lead you to better deal with these and with similar situations:

PRAYER: Father, when daily problems threaten to overwhelm me, help me to keep my eyes focused on You. Ease me out of my frustration with the comfort and guidance of Your presence.

Exercise 3

· · · · · · · · · · · · · · · ·

ANXIETY

Commit your way to the Lord; trust in Him and He will do this.
Psalm 37:5

*L*arry was a tall, blond, attractive, and very intelligent young man. When he first arrived on campus, every female student looked, whispered to her friend, giggled, or… tried to get his attention. Not only was he to become our top psychology major academically, but he promised to be a joy to have as a student. Inside and outside the classroom, Larry seemed, at first, to be a patient, kind, and gentle Christian witness to those around him. He expressed encouragement to others, was friendly and accepting of others.

Faculty and students alike gradually began to realize, however, that Larry demanded an academic perfection of himself that was unhealthy. Always the first at my office door after the most recent exam, he would want to know his grade immediately. My expressions of assurance that he had done well (he almost always made the top grade in the class) were not sufficient to relieve his anxiety.

"Don't worry!" I'd say, "We both know you did extremely well."

But he seemed driven to know that his work met and exceeded the expectations of his professors. I reassured Larry that doing his best was all that was expected of him. Still, he could never be at peace until he knew that his teachers were amazed with his outstanding performance. Although not an aggressive person, he would become angry over an exam or project if his work did not receive the highest grade in the class, complaining that the assignment was unfair or unclear or impossible. Eventually, this excessive anxiety began to annoy other students as well as faculty. Larry's anxiety, not only about exam grades but also about job applications, letters to graduate schools, and course papers seem to attach itself to everything he did. His fear of being a social outcast gradually became a self-fulfilling prophecy, and Larry couldn't understand why.

Anxiety often has its roots in a persistent attempt to manipulate and control others' opinions of us, especially if we've survived a troubled childhood. We can't bear to let other people hurt us as we've been hurt in the past and we try to prevent this repetition of hurt by controlling what they think of us. We are never able to control the perception of others, however, and our failure to control the way they see and react to us causes us great anxiety. Larry felt he must continue to be the best in every task to keep from being rejected by all, because otherwise they would see how worthless he really was. His perfectionism was an attempt to prevent others from verifying what his low self-esteem led him to believe about himself.

There are circumstances that frequently merit worry and anxiety, especially if God is left out of the picture. Concern and even anxiety may even be healthy if they relate to a specific situation and cause us to think about what we can do to make the situation better. We would be emotionally shallow if we weren't concerned about the sickness of a loved one, troubled by failure and financial burdens, or disturbed by unfairness and deception. Jesus wept tears at the death of a beloved friend.

When anxiety about what other people think of us pervades our lives, it's not an easy matter to surrender attempts to control their opinions. It involves hard choices and repeated efforts to let go and let God have complete control of our circumstances. The effort to manipulate and control others to avoid hurt may have become such an ingrained pattern of behavior that professional help or guidance by a Christian advisor is needed to break the cycle. Talk therapy over a period of time seems to be very beneficial for managing anxiety by promoting insight and constructive change in our choices and behaviors. But the anxiety caused by perpetuating this effort to control others' opinions is a self-defeating pattern of behavior and, as such, not in line with God's will for our lives.

God wants us to be governed by a quiet trust and sweet delight in Him. As we turn over our worries to Him and utilize the resources to which He directs us, God will help us to change. He will strengthen us and give us insight and wisdom. We can learn to face troubling situations with new vision and new confidence. Perhaps the very situation that caused us so much anxiety will be the springboard toward setting us more solidly on the path He wants us to take as we confidently walk with Him.

SPIRITUAL PREP: Psalm 37:3; Matthew 6:25–34; Mark 11:22–24; Luke 12:24; 1 Peter 5:7

Getting to Know Myself as a Child of God

Describe three situations, people, or things that make you really anxious or nervous:

Living as a Child of God

Now, lift each of these up to the Lord in prayer. Ask Him to take control of them and to guide you in dealing with each of them. Describe below what you think God would have you do about each situation:

**PRAYER: Father, don't let my life be controlled by worry or anxiety, but help me
to trust Your will in all my circumstances, knowing that You are in sovereign control.**

Exercise 4

· · · · · · · · · · · · · · · ·

ANGER

*The mind governed by the flesh is hostile to God; it does not submit to God's law,
nor can it do so. Those who are in the realm of the flesh cannot please God.*

Romans 8:7–8

Heather was such a pretty name for such an angry person! At the time I knew her, she worked in the administration office at college. Heather was angry at the world. Students couldn't bear her. Faculty disliked her. Other administrators and secretaries avoided her when possible, but she never acknowledged any anger. She always made a point of smiling at everyone she offended and often, since she was a minister's wife, ended frustrating encounters with students, faculty, and administrators alike with her practiced response, "God loves you!"

Heather's painful smile failed to mask a troubled, hostile person. She was the only one fooled by the smile. When a student made a valid complaint, Heather's response would inevitably be to deny the validity of the complaint or rationalize her own contributions to the problem. This she would do in a cold but calm voice and with the forced smile on her face. Yet her eyes betrayed her anger, and her words carried the intent of wounding the complainer. Heather and her husband, who had similar problems in the church where he ministered, took an early retirement right before I moved to a position at another campus. I don't think they ever resolved the anger issues that drove them both to an early retirement.

Anger is an authentic emotion. To simply deny its existence is unhealthy. While Scripture often addresses the issue of controlling unruly and inappropriate anger, God's Word also states that there is a place for the expression of authentic anger. "'In your anger do not sin': Do not let the sun go down while you are still angry, and do not give the devil a foothold" (Ephesians 4:26–27). It's no small accomplishment to be able to deal with one's anger in a manner becoming a Christian and constructive for those involved, especially if we were treated poorly as a child. But learning to express appropriate anger in an effective way increases our confidence and gives us a positive sense of self.

We don't want to betray ourselves by denying and avoiding anger at all costs. Nor do we want anger to become a constant, motivating force within us. It's an accepted medical fact that chronic anger and deep-seated hostility increase the risk of heart attack, cancer, and stress-related illnesses.

Chronic anger can result from several situations. Because emotional and physical mistreatment often offers children no liberty to express anger, they carry it, like a potential volcano, into adulthood, where it releases itself in explosive and destructive ways against those who hurt us. Chronic anger can also grow from an inability to control and confront, in a positive way, those who cause pain or violate us as adults. Christians are not exempt from either source of anger. Nor are we exempt from the need for professional help when anger reaches destructive proportions.

If you are struggling with anger, here's a tip that might help you: Try to locate the true source of your anger. Are you still responding to the hurts of childhood? Are you compromising yourself to gain the acceptance you desire? Are your beliefs, values, or trust being violated? Is your competence in question? Recognizing the actual fount of our anger can help us evaluate more clearly what currently does or doesn't merit our anger.

Even as we struggle to understand the reasons for our anger, our minds can begin to heal. In our daily walk with Him, we can ask Him to reveal the causes of our anger to us. Then as our eyes are opened, we can choose to release that anger, and the circumstances which trigger it, into His hands. We can set our minds on the joy of His presence in our lives and allow ourselves to drink in His blessings. With God's help and guidance, we can experience victory over chronic anger and nourished resentments.

SPIRITUAL PREP: Psalm 37:8; Proverbs 14:29; 15:1; Ecclesiastes 7:9; Ephesians 4:31–32; James 1:19–20

Getting to Know Myself as a Child of God

Think back for a while to your early childhood, and take the time to describe a situation which made you really angry:

How did you express your anger at this situation?

Living as a Child of God

If I could have anything I needed or wanted as I grew up, but didn't have, it would be:

PRAYER: Father God, teach me how to express appropriate anger. Show me the reasons
behind my anger when it's not appropriate, and help me to find healing for the source of that anger.

Exercise 5

· · · · · · · · · · · · · · · ·

NEGATIVISM

But no human being can tame the tongue. It is a restless evil, full of deadly poison. With the tongue we praise our Lord and Father, and with it we curse human beings, who have been made in God's likeness.

James 3:8–9

I've been a people-watcher all of my life. When dining with someone in a restaurant I make a poor dinner companion as my attention is distracted and then absorbed by those around me. Airports are mesmerizing. I often wait on a plane to arrive while sitting with a fixed gaze, charmed by the scene before me. People of all walks of life, ages, and cultures supply endless material for my imagination as planes land and take flight. This fascination with people has been a blessing as I've allowed God to minister through me to others. It also has a dark side: it can fuel a gossipy, critical nature. Gossip and criticism can destroy the object of their focus. They belittle rather than build up.

Lindsay recognized her own habit of perpetually gossiping and tearing down others' reputations. She wanted to change. I reassured her that she was well on her way to correcting the habit because she was aware of the habit, acknowledged it, and wanted to change! I was certain that her faith in God and willingness to follow His guidance would enable her to make the change she wanted. But because Lindsay was eager to take some immediate steps, I suggested a simple exercise to her. I told her to wear an elastic band around her wrist for a week. Each time she found herself gossiping or criticizing someone, she was to lightly snap her wrist.

After the week was up, she told me that the exercise helped a lot. However, she also came to realize that she would have to learn new ways of responding to others. With God's guidance and hard work, her efforts paid off. Over the next couple of years, Lindsay became one of the most positive and admired Christian leaders on campus.

I've seen gossip and criticism disguise themselves in the form of concern; they even dare to rear their ugly heads disguised as prayer requests. In the same breath that the Holy God was called upon, the person for whom prayer was requested was being slandered. Focusing on the spiritual shortcoming and sins of others generally reflects a lack of security—a need to see the weakness of others in order to feel good about one's own personality. If we've been trying to control the way others respond to us and they don't respond as we want, we may put bad thoughts and motives in their heads which are not really there. We then criticize and even slander them. Ignoble and petty criticism, judgment and condemnation of others, reflect a need to justify our own actions and see ourselves in a better position than the other person.

A negative, critical attitude does not emanate from a life controlled by Christ. God does not call us to attempt to control, judge and criticize; He calls us to listen, love, and encourage others. If Christ is truly

Lord of our lives so that our eyes are always focused on Him, then our attitudes will reflect acceptance of others and compassion for others. We will attempt to build up rather than tear down, strive for peace rather than cause disharmony, and seek unity rather than create division.

SPIRITUAL PREP: Psalms 34:13–14; 101:5; Proverbs 16:28; Matthew 7:1–5; Galatians 5:14–15; Ephesians 4:29

Getting to Know Myself as a Child of God

Sometime today, find and talk with at least three of your friends and/or family. Ask them to describe a time when they felt you've been negative about something or someone else. Take a notepad with you and jot down their responses. Before this day ends, record the responses of your three friends below.

Friend # 1 said I was negative when:

Friend # 2 said I was negative when:

Friend # 3 said I was negative when:

Living as a Child of God

Spend a few minutes in prayer, asking God to shed new light on these three situations and to show you alternative ways of looking at them. Record below anything that comes to mind:

PRAYER: Father, keep my mind and my tongue from gossip and criticism.
Help me to build others up rather than tear them down.

Exercise 6

· · · · · · · · · · · · · · · · ·

ACCEPTING RESPONSIBILITY FOR OUR ATTITUDES

For the Spirit God gave us does not make us timid,
but gives us power, love and self-discipline.
2 Timothy 1:7

Bitterness, anger, hopelessness, negativism, and other destructive emotions can infest the lives of those who have grown up in troubled families. Pretending all is well or blaming others for those emotions is not a healthy solution. Shawn was a bitter person. While she never pretended she was otherwise, she always found a cause or person to blame for her bitterness. "Isn't that awful about Ellen losing her son without being able to say good-bye to him," Shawn asked, restraining me with this question that was really a statement. I, too, felt deep sadness for Ellen who had heard second-hand of the death of her grown son. Before I could express my concern for Ellen, however, Shawn rushed on.

"I felt the same way Ellen felt when I heard that Nathan, my brother, had died. Nathan's wife is a real witch." Shawn continued as her face flushed with anger and her voice became even more vehement. "I'll certainly never forgive her for what she did! Do you know she wouldn't let me see Nathan at all during those last few months? What kind of person would prevent a sister from seeing her brother when he was dying?"

Shawn's face grew even more passionate and disturbed as she exclaimed how Nathan's wife had refused to talk to her after Nathan's death. Scarcely pausing for breath, words tumbled out of her mouth as anger flashed in her eyes. Shawn's struggle with bitterness and anger had existed before Nathan's death; but now, as always, the feelings had something concrete with which to attach themselves. The story of Nathan and his wife had been repeated to many people. The blaming words spilled out like water over a dam threatening to burst from the weight.

I attempted to calm the situation and suggested to Shawn that her bitterness seemed to be causing her a lot of pain. "No, it's not my bitterness that causes pain," she almost screamed. "It's that woman! If I could just tell her to her face what a witch she is, I'd be okay!"

Blaming others for our emotions gets us off the hook by making them responsible for what happens to us. It offers us some measure of relief, but the relief has a high price. The cost is loss of control over our own well-being. When we give up control of ourselves by blaming others, the result is increased anxiety, depression and a loss of sense of self.

Shawn was making herself ill with bitterness. As long as she blamed someone else for that bitterness, rightly or wrongly, she could not get better. The blame game perpetuates malcontent. It gets us nowhere in restoring healthy interpersonal relationships. To continue to take the perspective that someone or something else is to blame will only leave us powerless, resentful, and bitter.

Maturity means taking responsibility for ourselves: our thoughts, our emotions, our actions, and our reactions. It doesn't mean that the situation is our fault or that we caused it, but it does mean that we're taking the responsibility to respond, to take action—to *do* something about it.

Granted, assuming responsibility for our actions is easier to talk about than to do. However, we need to do more than just tell ourselves that we're going to accept responsibility, although that's a start in a healthy direction. We need to acknowledge to ourselves that beginning now, with God's help, we'll make it a point to accept responsibility for what we say and do. If we assume responsibility for our lives, our choices, our decisions, this will empower and free us. Our future is then what we want to make it. Our ultimate success will depend on us and not on the actions of others.

SPIRITUAL PREP: Ezekiel 18:20; Matthew 12:37; Romans 3:19–24; 14:12; Ephesians 4:31–32; Hebrews 12:14–15

Getting to Know Myself as a Child of God

This may be the most crucial part of your pilgrimage, so let's do some real (and perhaps difficult) work here. Dig deeply into your heart and mind, and describe one or more behaviors and/or emotions in your life for which you've blamed others:

Living as a Child of God

For just a minute, assume responsibility for these emotions and/or behaviors. How does that make you feel? What behavior changes in your life may you need to make, as a result? Ask God for clarity as you seek to answer these questions and write out any thoughts you have:

PRAYER: Father, free my heart from bitterness and blaming,
and help me to see the changes You desire me to make in my own life.

The Ashes of Destructive Relationships

Exercise 1

. . . .

SEARCH FOR THE MEANING OF LOVE

Then Mary took about a pint of pure nard, an expensive perfume;
she poured it on Jesus' feet and wiped his feet with her hair.
And the house was filled with the fragrance of the perfume.
John 12:3

Relationships are complicated! Even more so, relationships formed by individuals from troubled families may prove to be extremely difficult to maintain and enjoy. Whether it's friendship, professional relationships, or romantic relationships, these relationships are often characterized by conflict, fighting, and feelings of being misunderstood. If we anticipate the rejection we felt as a child, we may withdraw altogether before a relationship has had a chance to develop. Children from homes with inadequate parenting may not have had an opportunity to develop personal characteristics that are needed for a healthy, mature relationship. Some of these characteristics that may be lacking include self-confidence, trust, self-awareness, and assertiveness. Workshops or classes on interpersonal skills offered by a local community college, church, family service agency can help; however, even when we've developed the skills and the self-acceptance needed for a healthy relationship, there's no guarantee that love will be a story with a happy ending.

By working with others on significant relationships as well as dealing with relationships in my own life, God has helped me better understand the experience of loving and being loved. Still, even today, I recognize how difficult it can be to build a healthy, loving relationship. Love is a coming together of two separate but whole people. It is an interdependence, an emotional connectedness between two individuals who have distinct thoughts, feelings, and beliefs. It seeks the growth and expression of the God-given uniqueness of each party. It allows, even rejoices in, the freedom for each person to become all he or she can be, to share openly differing thoughts and feelings about important issues and to pursue avenues of growth that will encourage a more solid sense of "I" as well as "we" within the relationship.

Love means balance. It necessitates an honest understanding of what each is bringing to the relationship, so that neither person silences his or her own needs in order to meet the needs of the other. It involves clearly defining the roles, responsibilities, and limits of the relationship in a mutually acceptable and tolerable way.

Loving means becoming vulnerable. It means taking the risk of being honest so that the relationship is founded on reality rather than deception. It means caring enough to reveal differing perspectives in order to facilitate both one's own and the other's growth.

Love means committing ourselves to the beloved, for better or for worse. But commitment is far more than promising undying love. Commitment means keeping promises. It means being consistently there for the other person. It means creating a small island of security for each other. It means that you can be counted on. It means making space in your heart and life for the other, and to always be there no matter how crowded your life becomes.

Love is extravagant. It offers us a taste of heaven as we allow the great, unfathomable love of Christ to permeate our lives and our relationship with our beloved.

SPIRITUAL PREP: Song of Solomon 8:6; Romans 12:9; 1 Corinthians 13 (the whole chapter); Galatians 5:14; 1 John 4:12–18

Getting to Know Myself as a Child of God

Who was your best friend in elementary school?

Who was your best friend in high school?

Who was/is your worst enemy?

Who was your first crush?

Living as a Child of God

Who is the person with whom you feel most comfortable with sharing confidential information today? Who are the most precious people in your life today?

Think for a moment about what you'd like to tell each of the people who are most precious to you. Write it out below:

PRAYER: Father, help me to bring wholeness, balance, honesty, and commitment to each of my relationships.

Exercise 2

· · · · · · · · · · · · · · · ·

EMOTIONAL TRAPS

Come, all you who are thirsty, come to the waters; and you who have no money,
come, buy and eat! Come, buy wine and milk without money and without cost.

Isaiah 55:1

Laura never had the opportunity to form protective boundaries as a child. Her controlling parent gave her no privacy, no room to disagree, no space to develop a sense of self apart from them. Having reached her young adult years, Laura had failed to individuate or develop a definitive, separate sense of self. She continued to look to others, as she had to her parents, for her sense of personal identity. When she first reached beyond her family for a close, caring relationship, she did so unaware that she lacked the boundaries needed to separate her sense of self from others' opinions of her.

In her latest relationship, Laura had become dependent on her new friend, Jerry, to supply her need for esteem and feelings of worth. He became her world. His personality filled the tremendous gaps in her life. She felt whole and able to tackle any problem as long as Jerry was on her side. But if he disapproved of her thoughts or actions, or if she felt the slightest twinge of rejection, she was devastated.

Laura tolerated any criticism, excused any deception, accepted all guilt for any problem. She expended enormous amounts of energy, time, and effort to please Jerry and gain his approval. She pushed away her hurt and anger for fear of losing what little warmth remained. Laura believed broken promises and lies over and over, and forgave and forgot. She felt that, somehow, if she could just do enough, she would gain the love and attention from Jerry which validated her as a person of worth.

When she finally realized it was impossible to keep Jerry's love, Laura turned to God. In childlike trust, while the battle she could not win continued to rage, she asked God to help. God's love held steadfast. Laura and I spent many hours together as she established a sense of self and built her own healthy boundaries. It took time, but through the process of counseling, personal Bible study, and prayer, Laura began to see the destructive nature of her relationship with Jerry. God provided her with His peace, and helped her center her life on Him as she made the difficult decision to end the relationship with Jerry.

If you're involved in a self-perpetuating cycle of destructive relationships because you lack respect for your own or other people's boundaries, your challenge is twofold. You first need to work on developing a sense of self by defining who you are and what you believe. Then you may need to make some difficult choices.

Listen to your own needs and feelings. It will take time to build a sense of selfhood that tends its own boundaries and respects the boundaries of others.

Most importantly, listen to Jesus. He is the Living Water. He will satisfy your thirst for selfhood as you allow Him to guide you in setting boundaries. And far more than this: He will provide opportunities to form healthy relationships and transform your soul into a watered garden, as you learn to develop intimacies of *His* choosing.

SPIRITUAL PREP: Psalms 26:2-4; 36:7; Ecclesiastes 3:1, 8; Romans 8:37–39; Ephesians 2:4–6

Getting to Know Myself as a Child of God

Describe a destructive relationship in your life and why it was destructive:

Describe a relationship which comforted and encouraged you and what you think made it a healthy relationship:

Living as a Child of God

What kind of a relationship(s) are you looking for now?

Spend as much time as you need in prayer, asking God to examine your thoughts about the type of relationship(s) you desire—and to clarify what you, as a Christian, need in a relationship. Then, leave the request for that relationship in God's hands.

PRAYER: Lord Jesus, I need healthy, intimate relationships based on a solid sense of who I am.
I need to respect my own and others' limits. Help me to recognize and
appreciate the boundaries You've shown me that I need to place around my heart and life.

Exercise 3

. . . .

CONFLICT

Leave your gift there in front of the altar. First go and be reconciled to them;
then come and offer your gift.
Matthew 5:24

Regardless of how I planned and prayed about moments that demanded confrontation with a contemporary or a student, I always dreaded the task. Often I would break down in tears or feel uncontrollable anger welling up in me. Yet, I realized that confrontation was a necessary part of my work on campus, and I wanted to learn to do it with a Christian attitude.

Scripture provides several examples of confrontational situations. Genesis 32–33 tells how Jacob needed to confront his brother, Esau. Jacob was at fault, and Esau had the means to demand vindication if he so desired. Jacob needed to be forgiven by the brother from whom he had stolen a birthright. First Samuel 17 tells of a courageous young warrior, David, seeking to confront a legendary hero of the Philistine army who defied all Israel, Goliath. The common factor in both confrontations was the presence and guidance of God. It was within the strong interweaving of their lives with His will that both men realized their need for confrontation. They knew these were tasks they had to do. Jacob was afraid and admitted his fear. The innocent courage of David admitted no fear. But both men trusted God completely.

Give yourself time to think and pray before you confront. One of the most important tools in successful confrontation is to use the personal pronoun "I" to explain your feelings, rather than the accusatory "you." Let the other person know how you feel and what you want. As you tell the person why you're hurt or troubled, also let him or her know that you treasure the relationship and want the friendship to be restored. Aggression begets aggression. If you confront in a judgmental, blaming, nagging, complaining manner, you'll elicit disapproval and rejection more often than sympathy and change. Engaging in a cycle in which increasingly hurtful and angry remarks are traded will only result in a complete breakdown of communication. Also, make certain that your choice to confront another person is based on God's guidance and not on your own anger. Then set out—even if in fear, even if you're uncertain of what you'll say or do—to act on that guidance. With God as your guide, your effort will bring results that are best for you and for the person whom you're confronting. David slew his Goliath. Jacob found brotherly love.

Perhaps you'll stumble, and your efforts will not be well received. Perhaps you'll never be a hero nor find the resolution for which you hoped. But you will have the peace of knowing that you've done God's bidding; and the next time, when God calls you to confront another, you'll be more skilled and your walk with God will be the stronger for it.

SPIRITUAL PREP: Jeremiah 1:7–9; Acts 6:8–10; 2 Corinthians 5:18–19

Getting to Know Myself as a Child of God

Think back and remember a person or persons whom you've had to confront. Describe below what happened:

Living as a Child of God

Picture in your mind someone you need to confront now. Lift that person up to God and ask for God's guidance, then write out what you feel you need to say to him or to her:

PRAYER: Lord Jesus, give me the courage to confront when You lead.
Teach me to do so without accusation or aggression.

Exercise 4
· · · · · · · · · · · · · · · ·
FRIENDSHIP

Greater love has no one than this, that one lay down his life for his friends.
John 15:13 (NASB)

Meredith's right side hurt. It was one a.m. and I was afraid. "What can I do?" I thought. "I'm responsible for all twelve of these students and if Meredith has appendicitis, we need to get her to a hospital fast." But there was no hospital near the mountain retreat where we were staying, and the clinic at the retreat center had already closed.

"I know where a hospital is, and I'll be glad to ride with you there," said Kay. I had met Kay at the bookstore after the evening program. She was the featured singer during the retreat, and she had visited our cabin later to join my group's late-night devotions. Not only did all of my students immediately take to this warm, friendly Christian singer, so did I.

Together, Kay and I got Meredith into the car and headed out on the midnight-dark mountain road. Rain poured down furiously as I drove, and I became more and more afraid. Meredith, clutching her side in pain as she sat in the back seat, was crying. Sensing our fear, Kay reached into the back seat and clasped Meredith's hand in hers, as she began to quietly and calmly sing, "Learning to lean, learning to lean, I'm learning to lean on Jesus. . . ."

Meredith was diagnosed with having a stomach virus, and survived the ordeal with nothing more than a bad case of stomach cramps. Kay and I have since shared many of life's experiences together, and she has taught me much about the love of God. Twenty years later, I'm still blessed with the enduring friendship of this Christian lady.

While it's true that friends do favors for us and are there to help us when we need them, the real reason for friendship involves more than this. Lasting friends share their hearts' longing and find understanding. Lasting friends care unconditionally, so that each feels free to be himself in the other's presence. Lasting friends support and encourage each other.

"There are friends who pretend to be friends, but there is a friend who sticks closer than a brother" (Proverbs 18:24, RSV). A friend is not someone you use to fill your spare time or someone you claim as a friend only when he or she can be of some assistance or advantage to you. Friends are not disposable when you have more interesting social opportunities. Friendships based solely on utility lack the character needed to become enduring relationships.

Lasting friends enjoy our friendship—not because our friendship is a social advantage to them, but simply because they care. Lasting friends are loyal even when it costs them something. They make the effort to stay in touch, nourish the friendship, and remain faithful even when disappointment sets in. Lasting friends interrupt busy schedules to include each other and go the extra mile, if needed, for each other.

Lasting friendships are centered on God's love. They provide the opportunity for Him to love and minister to another through us.

SPIRITUAL PREP: Proverbs 17:17 18:24; 27:6, 10; John 15:13

Getting to Know Myself as a Child of God

List your friends in order of closeness. Then, beside each name, describe what you most like about each person:

Living as a Child of God

If possible, make a point of finding and spending some time today with each of the friends you just listed. Take a notepad and pencil with you. Ask each friend what he she likes about you. Take the time later today to record their answers here:

PRAYER: Lord Jesus, help me to be a true friend, to love unconditionally,
and to give priority to those whom You bring close to my heart.

Exercise 5

· · · · · · · · · · · · · · · ·

AUTHENTIC LOVE

Beloved, let us love one another, for love is from God;
and everyone who loves is born of God and knows God.
1 John 4:7 (NASB)

Barbara was one of my roommates in the Peace Corps. We were confident, strong-minded young adults and were certain we were part of an enlightened generation. As young people often are, we were skeptical of institutionalized religion and the hypocrisy that existed behind superficial expressions of Christian love. Barbara and I took pride in our conclusion that the enveloping love many Christians professed was impossible.

After Peace Corps, we went our separate ways. Barbara married and I, in an entirely different part of the world, entered graduate school. Shortly after marriage, Barbara lost her life to cancer. I truly hope she found God's love and grace before she died. I know that I continued to struggle with the concept of love, and the reality of it versus the illusion of it, for years. As a maturing adult, I often wondered if I could ever really obey God's command to love others.

There has never been an instantaneous transformation for me. It took many years for God to teach my stubborn heart to begin to love as He loves. But the awareness that He was changing my heart came one day during a quiet moment at the college where I later taught.

I sat at my desk despairing over my failure to win the friendship of one of my colleagues, Evelyn. My position required that I work closely with her, but Evelyn resisted any efforts to cooperate and twisted my motives for trying to do so. At a loss as to what to do, I decided to focus on ministering to my students and just leave my relationship with this colleague in God's hands. As the faces and personalities of my students came to mind—pretty, plain, bright, slow, motivated, or resentful—I realized that my heart was flooded with love for each one of them. I had always cared for my students throughout my teaching career, but never so purely, gently, and completely as I felt now. I knew, at that moment, that my love for my students was and always had been God's gift. I began to see that the love I felt for my students was the same love that I needed to express for my colleague.

Although I wasn't instantly able to love Evelyn, I realized that if I put this relationship in God's hands, He would eventually enable me to love this abrasive colleague. We never became close friends, but the spark of love that God placed in my heart at that moment did indeed grow until I was able to respond to Evelyn with the same affection I held for my students.

My roommate in the Peace Corps and I were right in our conclusion that it is humanly impossible to love every person we meet. Nonetheless, as I've permitted Christ to work in my life, to shape my thoughts, and to take control of the circumstances of my life, He has taught me to love even difficult people as He loves us. Christian, He who is in you is greater than he who is in the world. He who is in you *is* love. Trust Him. He will teach your heart to love.

SPIRITUAL PREP: Deuteronomy 10:12–13; Psalm 91:14; Luke 7:47; Romans 8:38–39; Jude 20–21

Getting to Know Myself as a Child of God

List three people who inspire you. What is inspirational about each person?

Now, think of one or more individuals who are difficult to like. What makes this person(s) difficult to like?

Living as a Child of God

Think again about the individuals whom you listed as difficult to like. How could you serve as an inspiration to these three individuals and learn to reach out to them with God's love?

PRAYER: Lord, teach me that You love me. Overflow my heart with Your love, and show me how to release that love to those around me.

Exercise 6

. . . .

LOVE LOST

But rejoice inasmuch as you participate in the sufferings of Christ,
so that you may be overjoyed when his glory is revealed.
1 Peter 4:13

Betty Ann's father's funeral was difficult for her, but not for the usual reasons. Betty Ann's father and mother had been emotionally estranged most of her life, with a lot of highs and lows in their marriage. Her dad was an alcoholic, and more often than not he seemed to follow a violent and self-destructive path despite the fact that he'd become a Christian earlier in life. Betty Ann told me many things that her father did to make his family ashamed of him, but Betty Ann suspected that her father hated these things even more than his family did.

Betty Ann told me she believed that if, in her father's youth, his childhood circumstances had been healthier, her father's life would have taken a different direction. There were times her father had been a kind, Christian man. One thing Betty Ann recalled was how her dad showed remarkable sensitivity to children and animals. This, Betty Ann said, forever left its imprint on her own life. But her father's gentleness turned to apathy and his kindness was destroyed by increasingly frequent alcohol binges. Her father's love for God and for his family was often marred by depression and anger. Betty Ann's father left home when she was a teenager, but he returned and reconciled with her mother after Betty Ann's graduation from college. He remained free of alcohol from that point on and attended church until his death a few years later.

At her dad's funeral, Betty Ann felt the shock and numbness of being severed from her father, but not the feelings which normally accompany mourning. There were no tears of loss, few regrets. The emotions which the termination of her father's troubled life brought were too tumultuous for Betty Ann to handle as a young woman. She kept all feelings at bay until years later, when nightmares and depression threatened to overwhelm her. Betty Ann was forced to seek help and, through counseling, was able to turn and confront the unresolved horror, fears, and anguish of this monster, death. In doing so, Betty Ann glimpsed the peace and beauty that accompany the transition from earth to eternity of a soul owned by Christ. "Where, O death, is your victory? Where O death, is your sting?" (1 Corinthians 15:55).

Perhaps you've lost some people you've loved but who have also hurt you. If they accepted Christ, it may make it even more difficult for you to understand how they lived the way they did—and their death left only unresolved mourning. But one day you will meet them again, and this time you will understand. Your questions will be answered, and you will see them as Christ meant them to be.

Betty Ann believes now that, in heaven, her father has finally began to walk, with his shoulders back and his head held high, in the direction that Christ beckons him to go. She knows that someday she will meet her father on that path and will find her dad a transformed man with the beauty of the heavenly Father in his face. Betty Ann has the assurance that she will experience the exquisite joy of sharing all eternity not only with her heavenly Father but also with the Daddy that life failed to offer.

SPIRITUAL PREP: John 5:24; 16:20; Romans 5:1–5; 6:9, 23; 8:28, 1 Corinthians 15:54–57

Getting to Know Myself as a Child of God

Whom have you loved and lost, either through death or through a broken relationship? How did you deal with that loss or losses?

Living as a Child of God

Think about and list one thing in each category which helps you deal with loss and sadness:

Music:

Books:

Places:

Animals:

People:

Scripture verse(s) (write it/them out):

PRAYER: Lord Jesus, I thank You for dying on the cross for me. Because You did,
I will once again be reunited and live in perfect relationship with those whom I love for all eternity.

Ashes When We Go Astray

Exercise 1

· · · · · · · · · · · · · · · ·

NEUROSIS

*Anyone who listens to the word but does not do what it says is like
someone who looks at his face in a mirror and, after looking at himself,
goes away and immediately forgets what he looks like.*
James 1:23–24

Although the word "neurosis" has long been replaced by more descriptive terms in the *American Diagnostic and Statistical Manual of Mental Disorders*, I continue to be asked, "Is sin caused by neurosis?" I've often thought about the relationship between the concept of sin and the concept of maladaptive or neurotic behavior. Unhealthy personality tendencies are sometimes related to a biological predisposition, a chemical imbalance, or a complex combination of both, but more often they are the results of early learning experiences. We do not choose these tendencies, nor is anyone totally free from maladaptive behaviors. None of us are perfect.

Addictive personalities are frequently the children of addictive personalities. Compulsive behavior in children may follow the pattern of compulsive behavior demonstrated by the parents. Abused children sometimes become abusive parents. We may have learned to greatly exaggerate truths, to become unreasonably jealous, to wallow in and waste away our lives in remorseful and negative thinking. We may consciously deceive others, use others to get our way, or feel we should always be the center of attention. We may recognize that we are almost always anxious, angry, or sad. We might see in ourselves tendencies to gossip and malign others, to seek sexual objects of an unhealthy nature, or to take advantage of the trust and honesty of others.

The good news is we don't have to perpetuate these patterns of behavior. That is a matter of choice. Neither learning, genetics, nor any combination of the two necessitate a lifetime behavior pattern. There may be a biological predisposition toward addictive behaviors, for example, but the choice must first be made to indulge in that to which one becomes addicted. Even after the addiction develops, each time we indulge we make a choice.

In every life, there comes a day of awareness. We recognize in ourselves those tendencies, those predispositions, those inclinations to behave in ways detrimental to our own well-being or to the well-being of those around us. When we become aware of these tendencies, we must consciously choose whether to act upon and indulge our unhealthy appetites or to make the effort to change that tendency.

It is at this point that we may face the most painful, difficult choice we'll ever have to make. At the point of awareness, the behavior we choose becomes our responsibility. Maladaptive behavior tendencies, in general, reflect the inherent, imperfect, sinful nature of man. I do not believe that God holds us personally responsible for our tendencies toward neurotic behaviors. I do believe, however, that when we become aware of our specific tendencies—and face the choice of either perpetuating them or doing something about them—that this is where our own personal sin begins or ends. It is at this point that God holds us personally responsible.

Accept that Jesus' death on the cross covers all confessed sin: original sin, which is part of our imperfect nature; and personal sin, which results from our own choices. It may take time, effort, and repeated failures to change. There might be a need to seek a wise counselor, support group, or a good friend through whom God can help us see life and options more clearly, but we need to begin. Surrender to God that which leads you to be less the new creation that He intends you to be, and He will help you make the right choices. He will send legions of angels to your side. The cycle can be broken.

SPIRITUAL PREP: Deuteronomy 30:19–20, Joshua 24:15; 1 Kings 18:21; Psalm 119:30; Luke 10:41–42

Getting to Know Myself as a Child of God

Describe a low point in your life, when you recognized you had an internal obstacle to living the Christian life:

Describe some steps you've taken, or plan to take, to overcome that obstacle:

Living as a Child of God

As you experience victories (no matter how small) over that internal obstacle, record those victories here:

PRAYER: Father, as I recognize those things in my life which can be changed,
guide me and give me strength to make the right choices.

Exercise 2

. . . .

RECOGNIZING PERSONAL SIN

*Those who cleanse themselves from the latter will be instruments for special
purposes, made holy, useful to the Master and prepared to do any good work.*
2 Timothy 2:21

Kevin came to me so distraught by his recent failure in the face of a particularly powerful temptation that he was ready to give up his plans to enter the ministry. He was a talented and intelligent, but lonely young man with only a small group of friends. In a desire to be accepted by the group, he had done something which he knew was not in God's will for his life. Kevin had tried to hide his mistake from his teachers and mentors and rationalize it to himself, but the awareness of it continued to haunt him until he could no longer excuse it. Kevin seemed devastated now by this failure and intensely felt that God expected better of him.

"I've never met a sinless person," I assured Kevin, and pointed that his distress showed how deeply he loved God and was evidence of the Holy Spirit working in his life. He acknowledged this with relief, and we went on to talk about his desperate need for acceptance by his friends and how this need might deflect him from his call to the ministry. We had several talk-sessions about Kevin's feelings of loneliness.

By grappling with his own loneliness and shyness, Kevin grew stronger in his sense of self and more confident in his own decisions. As he gained self-assurance, Kevin chose to remain true to His commitment to God and pursue his goal to become a minister. After graduation, Kevin entered seminary. In the last communication between us, Kevin was serving as the music and youth minister in a small church, and he and his sweet wife were expecting a new addition to their family.

We cannot fully grasp the meaning of being delivered from sin until we first recognize the horrible nature of sin that is in us. This realization comes for every individual in unique ways and does not necessitate a firsthand taste of the depravity of which we're capable. For some to realize this, however, God permits the potential for sin to become a reality. Whether we experience it firsthand or not, when we remain blind to the obvious horror of sin, we can only mouth, without substance, an appreciation for the purpose of Christ's death on the cross.

Denial, repression, and rationalization are all methods by which we shade our perceptions of our sin. It would be so much easier to pretend that we haven't sinned and to deny the reality of it both to ourselves and to God. We might try to repress sins from our memory without seeking His forgiveness. Frequently we rationalize our wrong choices by making excuses for them, blaming the other person, or claiming it couldn't have been otherwise.

In some manner, all of us must come to grips with the ugliness of our old nature without Christ. Once we're aware of sin and suffer the dismay of knowing that of which we're capable, we become responsible for our actions. Attempting to hide our choices and clinging to what we know to be sinful will only create personal misery, regardless of how much we feel we must have the secret thing. God, the Author of all truth, knows (as surely as any psychologist has surmised) that hiding reality from ourselves doesn't dissipate it. Instead, hidden sins ferment and call out for recognition and rectification.

When we experience the nagging guilt associated with sin, at least then we know that we have evidence of the Holy Spirit working in our lives. With His guidance, we can learn to distinguish between the deception of sin and the truth of God. If we allow this insight to create in us a hunger for more righteousness, a desire to be more like Him, and an inclination to sin less so that He needs forgive us less, then we are on the path toward assuming the new nature which is His gift to us. The path will not be easy. It will always be fraught with temptations. But Jesus will be there, picking us up when we fail, forgiving us, and pointing to a way free of sin. He will meet our needs abundantly.

SPIRITUAL PREP: Genesis 4:6–7; 2 Samuel 12:12–13; 1 Kings 8:46–50; Psalm 32:5; Romans 3:23; 1 John 1:5–10

Getting to Know Myself as a Child of God

Because of the importance of this step, this is being combined with the "Living as a Child of God" section. On the following page, you'll find the shape of a cross. Take a few minutes and think about any choices you've made which have been destructive to you—choices that you're now aware are outside the will of God. Using a pencil with a good eraser, lightly write—in code if you wish—each of these choices on the cross. As you write of each instance, lift up that choice in prayer to God and ask for His forgiveness. He will forgive you. Over the next few days, continue to pray about these choices, and when you're aware of God's forgiveness, take your eraser and erase each of those choices.

PRAYER: Lord Jesus, even as I ask You to bring me face to face with my sins, I also ask to know Your forgiveness and to feel clean and pure once again.

Exercise 3

. . . .

BREAKING THE MORAL LAW

Do not merely listen to the word, and so deceive yourselves. Do what it says.
James 1:22

What's the very worst thing you think you've ever done? Even though you may feel God's forgiveness for most of the sins in your life, does He seem to turn His face when you ask forgiveness for one particular act? Do you feel like you're leading a double life—that if anyone knew what an awful thing you'd done, they'd laugh in the face of your Christian witness?

At some point in our lives, we may feel that we've committed a sin so horrible that even God cannot forgive us. What we've done is more grotesque than we ever dreamed ourselves capable of doing. Yes, we reason, we've asked forgiveness, but perhaps we haven't been sincere enough in confessing the sin, or we just haven't used the right words! And because we think we cannot be forgiven, it becomes more and more difficult to forgive others of any sins they commit against us. The words of Matthew 6:12, "And forgive us our debts, as we also have forgiven our debtors," may seem to be an additional condemnation rather than a blessing.

Christian, take heart, and do not compare God's forgiveness to the human capacity to forgive. His forgiveness is like an infinite ocean which can remove and wash away *all* human acts, no matter how sinful. In recognizing your sin and your own capacity to commit it, you've already taken a great step. Christ's death on the cross is not in vain. His forgiveness runs deeper than any pit into which your choices and behaviors can plunge you. He asks only that you return to him, acknowledge your sin, and ask His forgiveness.

The greatest tragedy for a Christian is not the sin, although all sin is offensive to God. The greatest tragedy in life is the failure to admit sin and seek forgiveness. Some folks even try to justify sin and base the justification on partial spiritual truths. We mistreat our children in the name of "biblical" discipline; we intimidate our spouse and expect "scriptural" submissiveness; we oppress those with less strength and demand that they show "servant" obedience; we manipulate and deceive those with whom we live and expect "Christian" cooperation. We point our fingers at those who choose more obvious lifestyles of sin and start crusades against them, while ignoring our own sinful nature.

Once we make the choice to face our own personal sin, we're on the right track. Although we're often overwhelmed by the havoc sin has wreaked, it's never too late. It takes courage, openness, vulnerability, and sensitivity to admit the sin and make the choice to change. Oh, how His angels must rejoice when we face and acknowledge our sin, no matter how awful it may seem to us. Once our sin is acknowledged, confessed, and forgiven, it is no longer impossible to forgive others. We are able to draw from the great reservoir of His forgiveness and cleansing in our own lives.

Claim the forgiveness given to you when Christ died on the cross, and ask God to free your mind from the suggestion that your sin is somehow unforgivable. Reject the image, once you've confessed your sin, that God turns His face from you. Accept His perfect love and the new beginning He gives. A doer of the word sees his or her face in the clear reality of God's truth, and in that insight, chooses to turn from the sin. And "they will be blessed in what they do" (James 1:25). Claim the blessing and turn to look, freed from sin, fully into the face of a loving God.

SPIRITUAL PREP: Psalm 90:8; Proverbs 28:13; Isaiah 1:18–20; Jeremiah 33:8;
Mark 3:28; Acts 13:38–39; Hebrews 10:17

Getting to Know Myself as a Child of God

Describe an instance where you forgave someone for a sin they committed against you:

Describe a situation where someone forgave a sin which you committed against them:

Living as a Child of God

On the cross from the previous exercise, write (again, in pencil) a description of the sin that you find the hardest to forgive in your life. Take a few moments and confess this sin to Christ. Ask His forgiveness, wait a few moments in silent prayer, and then erase the sin. If you find yourself returning to this sin (no matter how many times), again write it on the cross, asking Him to forgive you and to give you strength to turn from that sin.

PRAYER: Lord Jesus, teach me that there are no sins too large for You to forgive.
Provide the courage and the guidance I need to change my sinful ways.

Exercise 4

· · · · · · · · · · · · · · · ·

FORGIVENESS

The steadfast love of the LORD never ceases, his mercies never come to an end;
they are new every morning; great is thy faithfulness.
Lamentations 3:22–23 (RSV)

If God loved only sinless saints, we would all be left out in the cold. He loves sin-stained persons too. God so loved sinners—you and I—that He sent His Son to take our punishment by suffering and dying on the cross for us. Immediately, when we recognize this fact and accept as our personal redemption His death on the cross for us, we are forgiven.

Seeking forgiveness of sin is not an easy task. It can include a lot of anguish. On the other hand, confession and seeking forgiveness promote health of both mind and body. Only when we seek God's forgiveness can our minds and hearts be cleansed. The death of God's Son redeemed us from all sin—past, present, and future. We need not allow our failures to drag us down into despair and incapacitate our efforts to serve Him. We need not feel that we're doomed to suffer miserable circumstances for each sin we commit. As quickly as we admit our sin and ask His forgiveness, we're forgiven.

Despair and guilt and unhappiness are not the fulfillment of the promises of His word. If we're not bent on punishing ourselves ten times over for every sin we commit, then a life of service to Him can produce a joy and a confidence that nothing else offers. We'll never achieve perfection in this life, nor will we escape the suffering that we bring on ourselves. But if God lives in our hearts, we can meet every circumstance and overcome every sin with incorruptible confidence because we belong to Him.

When we awaken in the morning, His mercies are fresh with us! When we become busily involved in our day, His care remains over us. As we retire in the evening, he is still minding us, calling us to seek His companionship, His forgiveness.

As your day stretches on, remember to keep a short account with your Heavenly Father. Immediately confess your sins and seek His forgiveness. Then a big, long list never needs to build up. Remember, it is the love of God for sin-stained persons that is creating tomorrow's saints.

SPIRITUAL PREP: 1 Corinthians 6:11; 2 Corinthians 5:21; Colossians 1:21–23; 1 John 1:9

Getting to Know Myself as a Child of God

Describe the relief which you feel from the forgiveness of any past sin you've placed on the cross so far:

Living as a Child of God

Ask God for guidance as you think about forgiving yourself of sins. Describe how you can continue putting this into practice:

PRAYER: Lord Jesus, how wonderful to know that every morning brings a fresh, new supply of Your mercies and Your forgiveness.

Ashes After Life's Blows

Exercise 1

. . . .

TRIALS BY FIRE

*I will restore the fortunes of my people Israel, and they shall rebuild
the ruined cities and inhabit them; they shall plant vineyards and drink their
wine, and they shall make gardens and eat their fruit.*
Amos 9:14 (RSV)

We're concerned that, with your hearing loss, you won't be able to learn the language of another country," Dr. Wolf, the Medical Director of the Foreign Mission Board, said. I became defensive. I had easily made it into the Peace Corps a few years before, and that was a more strenuous evaluation process! Why shouldn't I just as easily make it through a foreign mission appointment?

"But I learned the language in the Philippines," I replied.

"Did you become fluent in Filipino?" he asked.

"Well, no," I responded, "but that's just because I don't learn languages easily."

"You have difficulty learning because you're unable to hear the subtleties of the language when it's spoken," he said. "Besides, there's something else."

"What?" I began to be alarmed.

"You have a heart murmur," he replied. "It's fairly common, but we did lose a missionary with a similar heart murmur a few years ago."

I was young and enthusiastic, and I felt I knew without a shadow of a doubt that I was to be a foreign missionary. Now the lifelong dream crumbled around my feet, and I faced the first real trial of faith in my young life.

Shadrach, Meshach, and Abednego, in the book of Daniel, experienced a literal trial of faith by fire when they refused to heed the call to worship false gods. Although perhaps not as literal, we as Christians will experience many trials of faith during our lifetimes. The world will beckon us, and our beliefs will be tested.

As new Christians we determine to yield our lives to God believing, like Shadrach, Meshach, and Abed-nego, that we will be true even when it means suffering. Then, when things don't go the way we plan and we actually experience failure, we question. We may cast ourselves on Him, expecting God to remove us from the fire and clear the obstacles in our path. When He doesn't, when the path remains blocked, we begin to doubt and wonder if God really cares about us. We're too shortsighted to see the results of the trials He allows to touch our lives; we scoff and scorn our faith, threaten to give up, pout and sulk, and even despair. Perhaps we would discard our faith altogether if it weren't for the insistent tug on our hearts by the Holy Spirit.

Shadrach, Meshach, and Abednego walked from the furnace untouched by the flames of death. The only thing that burned was the cords that bound them. Christian, hang on. You, too, will eventually walk triumphantly from the valley of suffering and stand resurrected in the newness of your life in Christ. And you will know more of Him, as well as of the direction He wants for your life, for having walked through the flames.

SPIRITUAL PREP: Psalm 121:1–4; Zephaniah 3:17; John 16:33; 2 Corinthians 1:5; 1 Peter 1:6–7

Getting to Know Myself as a Child of God

Describe three instances where you experienced a trial by fire. Where do you think God was, in each of those trials?

Living as a Child of God

If you're in the midst of a trial by fire and have yet to escape, think how you might be victorious. Pray about this and allow God to help you find your answers. Write your prayer below.

PRAYER: Father God, make Your presence known to me, when I go through the trial of faith produced by events which have not progressed as I'd hoped and planned.

Exercise 2

. . . .

PERSECUTION

They will have no fear of bad news;
their hearts are steadfast, trusting in the Lord.
Psalm 112:7

While serving as a campus minister early in my career, I encountered a charming professor of psychology who expressed a strong distaste for Christians and Christianity. Dr. Manley attacked Christian beliefs and labeled them the source of wars as well as the cause of most of the world's ills. One of his favorite illustrations was the story of a misguided mother he'd known who refused to let her terminally ill son be operated on because she believed the child could be healed by faith. The son later died. Dr. Manley told this story repeatedly, as well as one about a father who perversely claimed, as his Christian right, the submissive acceptance by his daughter of his sexual overtures.

How tragic that these examples exist and exist in abundance. But Dr. Manley, wanting to find the cause for the pain with which he daily counseled, placed all the blame squarely on the shoulders of Christianity. Christian beliefs, as he perceived them, were distorted and sick. Dr. Manley felt it was his duty to eradicate any such beliefs from the minds of his students and, in doing so, launched a concerted attack on Christian faith. Often the persecution to which Christians are subjected by the world is a very subtle, undercutting pressure, such as that experienced by Christian students in Dr. Manley's classes and counseling sessions. The persecution takes the form of a slight put-down, a barely perceptible smirk, or a joke at the Christian's expense. It ostracizes, intimidates, and ignores.

Even as Christians, our human nature can lead us to think up some spectacularly malicious deeds against fellow Christians. We spread rumors, even enhance them, and ruin a life forever. We exclude those who do not believe exactly like we do—or, even worse, we judge them to be un-Christian without even knowing their hearts. We deny others places of service based on race, gender, or social standing. If that happens, if we're the ones being victimized by someone claiming to be a Christian, the persecution seems even more difficult to bear.

In love, Christian, when you feel persecuted, I ask you to examine your intentions. Make certain that you are not the persecutor. And if you are made a victim of persecution, snuggle close to the heart of Christ. Instead of plotting revenge on your tormentors, seek God's comfort. Trust Him to take care of all of your circumstances, and He will direct your response. He will calm and strengthen you, and give peace to your heart. He will show you how to deal with the persecution without seeking revenge. To rest in His peace, without seeking retaliation, knowing that God is in control even in the midst of persecution, is the truest form of humility.

SPIRITUAL PREP: Psalms 7:1-2, Matthew 5:10, John 15:20-21, I Corinthians 4:12-13,
I Peter 4:14-19, Romans 12:19-20

Getting to Know Myself as a Child of God

List and describe any persecutions you've had to endure:

Living as a Child of God

Think about how you reacted to each of the above instances of persecution. How did they affect your Christian walk? Describe how they might (or did) strengthen your walk with God.

PRAYER: Father, give me the strength and peace of mind I need to endure persecution from others without retaliation. Above all, Lord Jesus, show me if I'm the persecutor—and if I am, forgive me.

Exercise 3

· · · · · · · · · · · · · · · ·

LOSS

*When you pass through the waters, I will be with you; and when you pass
through the rivers, they will not sweep over you. When you walk through the fire,
you will not be burned; the flames will not set you ablaze.*

Isaiah 43:2

*I*t was an early Sunday evening. As I sat in a pew of an almost empty church waiting for the program to begin, the late afternoon sun crept soft and warm through the stained glass windows, dumping its golden rays in my lap. The program that evening was a film which told a story of a young boy who was dying of cancer.

The boy's mother, to take his mind off of his suffering, told him to listen for the bells of heaven which Jesus would ring for him when it was time to join Him in heaven. When the end came and the small boy was in intense pain, the medical attendants were baffled by his smiles and puzzled by his frequent references to the bells. Later they asked the mother about this. She explained that her child had only heard the bells of heaven welcoming him home.

There are times when all of us will face physical or emotional events that trigger a despair which seems unbearable. On some of those occasions, we may feel completely alone. It might seem like there's no one with whom we can share our sorrow. We can't even reach the bottom of our hurt, but we sense its depth and it frightens us. Our cries to God may seem to fall cold at our feet; and at those times we may sense in ourselves the capacity to grow bitter and angry and turn away from God. "Where are You, Lord, when I can't see Your face?" we ask. "Why do You remain silent when I try so hard to hear you?" In these times, it may be helpful to reach out to a pastor, a Sunday school teacher, or spiritual leader who will be supportive and understanding. Don't hesitate to seek out such a person who is caring and sympathetic to your pain.

God's silence can be an opportunity for growth and a deeper understanding of Him. Sometimes His silence is actually His answer. He trusts you to keep faith while He prepares an even bigger revelation of Himself or brings you to a fulfillment of His purposes for your life. God allowed silence for three days before raising Lazarus. Is He allowing a period of silence in your life for a reason? Is there an answer to be found in His silence? Remember, His is a still, small voice and we may need to listen closely to hear His voice in the silence.

As I watched the film that Sunday evening, I remembered how God's bells had rung for me at difficult times. When problems loom too large for you to solve and all you feel from God is silence, stop a moment. Listen. There may be bells from heaven for you also.

SPIRITUAL PREP: Psalms 23:4; 34:18; Isaiah 49:13; Matthew 5:4; 2 Thessalonians 2:16–17

Getting to Know Myself as a Child of God

Describe a problem in your life, current or from childhood, which threatens/ed to overwhelm you:

Living as a Child of God

Take a few minutes and lift the above situation up in prayer to God. Wait and listen silently for His comfort and guidance. If you feel that He's given specific guidance to you during your prayer time, describe it below:

PRAYER: Father, when I'm in pain, help me to stop and listen for the music of heaven's bells.

Exercise 4

· · · · · · · · · · · · · · · · ·

FINDING COURAGE TO CONTINUE

Therefore, my dear brothers and sisters, stand firm. Let nothing move you.
Always give yourselves fully to the work of the Lord,
because you know that your labor in the Lord is not in vain.
1 Corinthians 15:58

George had just accepted his first teaching position at the college where I taught. His new department chair, Allen, seemed to be a dynamic Christian—so full of life that George felt they would make a marvelous ministry team. He thought working for Allen would be a joy and a privilege. A whirlwind of unpacking, preparing materials for rapidly approaching classes, and helping his new wife settle into a temporary apartment all accompanied his move to this place.

A small house, more like a little cottage, with ample room for a couple, caught George's eye. It was owned by the college and he could purchase it, if he would do the needed repairs, at a very reasonable price. Several of his colleagues and some of his ministerial students offered to help him do the painting, refinishing, and carpentry needed to make the house livable.

Being reassured by his co-teachers that the cottage was available, he inquired in our college's business office about the procedure involved. Sadly, he learned that the business manager with whom he'd have to deal didn't really want the house sold. George found himself repeatedly blocked, delayed, and manipulated. The manager would fail to keep appointments, allow deadlines with lawyers to pass, and scold George for inquiring into the things that needed to be done. What a way to begin his life in this new location!

But that was only the beginning. Gradually, George's frustration reached an emotional peak and he confided in Allen about the problems he was having. Allen's reaction was cold and unsympathetic. The business manager and Allen had professional ties, and Allen didn't wish to offend this nor any administrator.

George eventually was able to purchase and move into the small house and settle into his new teaching position. He was a remarkable teacher, but as his reputation grew more positive among his students, the relationship between him and Allen became brittle. George became the victim of manipulation and deception by Allen and the business manager. Even though Allen encouraged differing opinions, if George disagreed with him, however gently, his views were deemed unacceptable. George was given poor evaluations by Allen and left out of crucial departmental meetings. He was overlooked for departmental luncheons and holiday gatherings. Although I taught in a different department, I was grateful but surprised when this enthusiastic young professor accepted a second year's contract at our school.

Eventually, Allen and the business manager moved on to a different school while George remained with us. A few years later, George and I were talking about his early rough years at our college, and I asked him how he endured all that had happened. George told me that it was actually one of the most spiritually strengthening times of his life. During, and because of, the continual conflicts he began to see far better what it meant to walk alone with God. He grasped and cherished the belief that in God's eyes, his work wasn't in vain. During the days, weeks, and months spent in these circumstances, George took refuge in God's strength and love as he poured out desperate prayers that God would keep him safe and secure.

A Christian is not immune to gossip and slander! In spite of our best intentions, our efforts will sometimes be misunderstood, ignored, or even deliberately misrepresented. Instead of praise and recognition, we may encounter hostility, jealousy, and petty schemes to undermine what we do. During these times, the real test is whether or not we can remain steadfast in our faith and receptive to the Holy Spirit. George didn't feel that he always lived up to that test, but he kept trying to walk with, talk to, and listen to God. Eventually, he was able to see how God worked through his circumstances.

Through all situations, no matter how difficult, cling to God. He will guide your steps as you labor to serve Him.

SPIRITUAL PREP: Psalms 18:31-33, Psalms 27:1, Psalms 46:1-3, Psalms 91:11-12, Isaiah 26:3-4; Galatians 6:9; II Timothy 1:12

Getting to Know Myself as a Child of God

Describe an instance when your actions were misinterpreted or misunderstood. Who were the person(s) involved? How did it make you feel?

Living as a Child of God

Take a few minutes, now, and lift those persons involved up to the Lord, asking Him to help you forgive them and to show you how to react to them. If any specific thoughts come to mind, write them down.

PRAYER: Lord, help me to persevere. Help me keep my eyes on You, not on what others say about me. Give me a courageous, forgiving heart as I try to do Your will.

Exercise 5

· · · · · · · · · · · · · · · · ·

VICTOR, NOT VICTIM

He tends his flock like a shepherd: He gathers the lambs in his arms and carries
them close to his heart; he gently leads those that have young.
Isaiah 40:11

The mosquitoes were eating me alive. Their bites left red, angry bites that made me look like I had the measles. The situation was made even more unbearable by the heat. With no electricity, no fan, and no air-conditioning, my body cooled itself by sweating—and the perspiration only made the itching more ferocious.

In the dry, hot Filipino town, there was no glass for windows nor window screens available; the rough homes were built with large gaps for windows so that the residents could catch any outside breeze. The other Peace Corps volunteers and I put up screening sent from Peace Corps headquarters, choosing to suffer heat rather than insects. Still, we shared our living quarters with many of these insects, and they were in abundance: spiders, roaches, mosquitoes, as well as small lizards.

In addition to being plagued by insects, our efforts to keep a budget were a complete failure. The Peace Corps gave each volunteer an allowance in Filipino currency which matched the income of a native Filipino teacher. My roommate, Sandy, and I had not managed to make it through a single month on our allowance since arriving in the Philippines. The last week of this month was typical, and we were hungry. While discussing what we could do this month, the wife of a missionary stationed in our small town knocked on our screen door and invited us for the evening meal. This became a repeated pattern as other individuals, unknown to each other but friends with Sandy and I, would invite us to meals or drop off fresh fruit or produce which sustained us through many an end-of-the-month small hunger crisis.

As I look back, I realize that I matured more during that period of having to survive the difficult monthly budget problems than at any earlier time in life. Uncertain circumstances taught me to look to God for strength. Sandy and I still tried to solve our budget problems ourselves, but I came to intensely value the moment-by-moment guidance from God. I learned to rest my anxieties on Him believing—although perhaps not feeling it at the moment—that He would take care of me. These difficult times, more than anything else, taught me to walk by faith.

It's surprising how hardships can teach us to sing and how, through troubling times, we can start to grasp the deepest emotions of our own soul. The sweetest solace that can be known is the touch of God's hand in the midst of difficult, even terrible, circumstances. When we are so weighed down that we're unable to take a step in any direction, He carries us, sometimes without our knowing it, in His bosom like a shepherd gathering His lambs.

Christian, if only we could see as God sees, perhaps we would recognize the potential for growth that adversity provides. Just as Christ won the victory over suffering on the cross, so can we, through our faith in Him, become victors over suffering rather than victims.

Spiritual Prep: Psalms 27:5; 46:1; Romans 5:3; 8:17; 1 Peter 3:14–17; 4:16; 5:10

Getting to Know Myself as a Child of God

Write a story of a time when you experienced victory over suffering and describe how you grew from that experience:

Living as a Child of God

Is there a miracle that you'd like to see performed in your life? If so, describe it below. Then, lift it up to God in prayer, expecting Him to answer. Write your prayer below as well.

PRAYER: Lord Jesus, help me to recognize the touch of Your hand when circumstances become difficult and seem unbearable. Allow me to rest my anxieties on You and to learn the lessons You want me to learn from this experience.

Section Two

Rising from the Ashes

The Phoenix Rises

Exercise 1

. . . .

FAITH INTERNALIZED

But now, by dying to what once bound us, we have been released from the law so that we serve in the new way of the Spirit, and not in the old way of the written code.
Romans 7:6

I know what I believe!" Malcolm exclaimed.

Malcolm had applied for work on the mission field, but his application had just been turned down by Reverend Martin; and now, Malcolm expressed his hurt at the "accusations" he'd just heard from the pastor.

"No," Rev. Martin responded, "You *think* you know what you believe, but your beliefs are those of your parents. You wear them as a cloak. You've never been allowed to think for yourself. You've not internalized what you believe and don't believe. If you ever encounter a difficult situation, your beliefs will not stand the test. They are too superficial."

Malcolm was angry. It was only later, after living on his own, that Malcolm realized the validity of what Rev. Martin had told him.

Internalization of faith occurs when we're allowed to think for ourselves. Throughout childhood, and especially in adolescence, we embark on a passionate pilgrimage to define a separate and whole "I." Questioning and exploring alternative ways of perceiving life become a part of the pilgrimage. For the most part, the strong beliefs taught to us will be adopted, but some may be discarded as we learn to think for ourselves.

Especially during the adolescent years, young people need to be encouraged to think for themselves and form their own opinions, even if they don't agree with adults in charge. More and more, they need the freedom to experience the consequences of the decisions that they make. Sometimes this may appear to be rebellion toward the parents or the teacher, but there's a difference between healthy rebellion—when a child begins to think for himself—and unhealthy rebellion. Disagreements may arise, but the wise parent or teacher knows how to ride the waves of disagreement rather than react punitively, as the young person struggles to find answers. Listening, calm discussion, and unconditional love guide the rebellion into mature thinking.

As a young adult, Malcolm still faced the adolescent task of forming a solid sense of self, including those beliefs for which he would live—or yes, even die. Growing up under the sheltered roof of an authoritarian, punitive father and homeschooled by a strongly opinionated mother, the fear of consequences which had guided him as a child was no longer sufficient. Heeding the voices of what he'd been taught or following the natural inclinations of his own heart became a persistent dilemma in his search for what he believed. Going away to college, finding a job, and taking advantage of opportunities which God provided to experience lifestyles different from his own sheltered existence furthered his quest for an authentic sense of self, but he made some serious mistakes along the way.

Now remorseful of those mistakes, Malcolm realized that what Rev. Martin had told him so long ago was true. Desperate to find a faith of his own, Malcolm began attending a church more regularly and participating in a Bible study group. Most important, he maintained a daily quiet time with God. That quiet time became essential to Malcolm's efforts to distinguish God's voice more clearly. The childhood cloak of obedience gave way to a heart filled with gratitude and a desire to please his Lord. Malcolm eventually found a new mission field and God has blessed him richly. He continues to teach and minister to students in the college where he is now employed with a strong, sustaining faith in God.

SPIRITUAL PREP: Proverbs 4:18; Ephesians 4:13–15; Philippians 1:6–10; Colossians 1:9–12; 1 Peter 2:2–5

Getting to Know Myself as a Child of God

How have your beliefs changed from those you were taught and adopted as a child? Describe those changes below:

Living as a Child of God

Describe ten beliefs about life and God which you hold dear enough to live or die for. Number them as you list them.

PRAYER: Keep me growing, Lord. Keep me open to new experiences and new ways of looking at life as You guide me and help me to develop a mature, stable faith. Help me discern between error and Your truth.

Exercise 2

. . . .

LIVING LIFE WITH FAITH

If you remain in me and my words remain in you,
ask whatever you wish, and it will be done for you.

John 15:7

Tracy, a bright, engaging student, was telling me why she refused an invitation from a young man on campus to go to a local bar. She described how she felt a "no" from God when the thought of this invitation came to mind during her morning devotional time. Tracy said that before realizing how much God cared about every detail of her life, she had never expected Him to make Himself known to her in anything less than monumental events. She believed that He couldn't be bothered with the trite encounters of her boring routine, so she went about her way, floundering in her own ineptness to meet the demands made upon her daily.

It was out of repeated failure, Tracy said, that she began to depend upon God in all matters, not just major decisions. As she did so, He showed her that He would, indeed, make His presence known to her in the details and small decisions she faced daily. Tracy described how she began to expect exciting results from praying about even the routine things in her life. A whole new world opened up to her. When problem situations, no matter how significant or insignificant, engulfed her and dark clouds momentarily lingered over her head, she became aware of His presence, guiding her and restoring clarity to the situation and confidence to her walk.

What joy this new discovery brought to Tracy! What a beautiful, new relationship with Him! As she attempted to listen for and abide by the guidance He gave in these lesser moments, He seemed to move within her heart and reconcile her life more and more to Him. Gradually, in the conscious awareness of lifting up day-by-day events to Him, Tracy told me, God took the rough, protective shell behind which she often hid and gently released all that was creative and bright in her. In small ways and seemingly insignificant moments, He taught her to love in a whole new way. If she had never grasped this lesson of giving Him the little details of her life, Tracy added, she shuddered to think how she would have missed knowing the riches of His abiding presence in all areas of her life.

God cares about small things. He cares about the meeting you're going to have with the co-worker, the lunch date you have with a friend, even what you'll talk about at that lunch. He cares about the music you choose, the movie you and your friend see, and whether or not you buy that new outfit. Learn to trust Him with those small things and then watch! Through such daily trust, you'll see Him do much bigger things as well.

SPIRITUAL PREP: Psalm 37:23–24; Proverbs 16:9; Isaiah 58:11; Luke 12:6–7

Getting to Know Myself as a Child of God

List some of the major decisions which God has led you to make in your life:

Living as a Child of God

Now, take a few moments to think through the past twenty-four-plus hours, beginning with when you woke up yesterday. List all the details in that period of time, no matter how small, about which you think God cared and why.

PRAYER: Father, help me to listen for Your still, calm voice as You guide me in all the events which make up my day. Let me know that nothing is too small to bring to You for Your care and guidance.

Exercise 3

· · · · · · · · · · · · · · · · ·

INVESTING IN THE RIGHT THINGS

When Jesus heard this, he said to him, "You still lack one thing.
Sell everything you have and give to the poor, and you will have treasure
in heaven. Then come, follow me."
Luke 18:22

"But I'm the one who's poor," Jason blurted out as he repeated the above Scripture verse from his morning reading. Surviving on a part-time income while attending a small but expensive Christian college left Jason feeling that he was the poor person in need. "Why did God give me this to read?" he asked. Jason exclaimed that he certainly didn't have to worry about being too wealthy to enter the kingdom of God! Poverty had lately been a fast companion.

As our discussion of this Scripture passage continued, Jason began to realize that he was not poor by any stretch of the imagination. His needs were adequately met; his medical bills were paid by his parents' insurance; there was always food on his table; and he was even able to give a small amount to his church. True, he had few luxuries, but he wasn't poor in the real sense of the word. Digging deeper into his thoughts, Jason expressed gratitude for his part-time employment, family, friends, bright sunshine days, and studies at the college. He recognized that he had a church family that loved him and friends who inspired and uplifted him. He laughingly mentioned that he and his housemates had two fat, furry cats that purred and bounced on their laps whenever they had the chance and a sheepdog who misdirected his herding instinct toward the cats. And, Jason added, he had a clear mind and God-given insights. Suddenly, Jason was smiling at the abundance of riches in his life.

There are no possessions, no human relationships, no positions, no honors that we can obtain which will ever earn us one second of time in God's presence. There is nothing earthly that will create a more Christlike nature within us. There is nothing that will ever exceed the joy of knowing Him, nor hold more purpose than serving Him.

It is a joyful day when our thoughts are no longer dominated by concern for earthly treasures—when our hearts seek first and always His kingdom and His righteousness. It's difficult for the rich man to enter the kingdom of God—the man who is rich in friends, in family, in prestige, in position, in being a part of a culture that offers so many material pleasures—because his mind is more often preoccupied with those things than with the God Who gave those blessings to him. Only by placing our faith and hope in our Lord will we ever know the riches of being a part of His kingdom.

SPIRITUAL PREP: Proverbs 10:2, 22; Malachi 3:10; Matthew 6:19–21; 19:20–21; Luke 12:15; 2 Corinthians 9:8

Getting to Know Myself as a Child of God

Which of your possessions are most important to you?

Take a few minutes and talk with God about those things that are important to you and ask Him if they are possessions He wants you to have in your life. Describe how you think God responds to your possessions.

Living as a Child of God

Make a list of many blessings as you can which God has given you:

PRAYER: Lord Jesus, You have blessed my life so abundantly! But the greatest blessing of all is Your companionship. Thank You for making me rich in what really counts.

Exercise 4

· · · · · · · · · · · · · · · · ·

FAITH VERSUS SELF-WILL

A brother wronged is more unyielding than a fortified city;
disputes are like the barred gates of a citadel.
Proverbs 18:19

The students involved in our campus ministry program decided to have an all-day evangelism emphasis on campus. Their goals were high, their dreams glorious, and their enthusiasm unlimited. They'd invited some eminent personalities to be part of the day's program and, although they'd not yet raised the necessary funds, the personalities had accepted.

Brandon, the campus minister, wasn't at peace about the concentration of effort and funds the students had put into this one day's event, but decided to support their plans. He hoped the enthusiasm elicited by this event would result in spin-off ministries that would fulfill a vision of campus prayer groups, discipleship training, and year-long evangelism. Once the decision was made to support the all-day program, he became caught up in the plans of the students and the high hopes they had of "reaching the campus for Christ." He was totally unaware that trouble was about to begin.

In the midst of the clamor and busy preparation for this day, he answered his telephone one morning and found himself listening to an admonition from the minister of one of the larger churches in town. The financial contribution of the minister's church was vital for Brandon's entire campus ministry program as well as for the special day's events the students were planning. The minister of this church objected strongly to the stance of one of the personalities invited. In fact, he threatened removal of his support of the entire campus ministry if this person was not removed from the program.

Angered by the minister's authoritarian tone, Brandon refused to give in to his demands. Neither the minister nor Brandon were willing to sit and discuss the issue and consider the views of the other. The disagreement reached others who tried to negotiate with both the minister and with Brandon, but their respective egos prevailed. Much later, Brandon admitted that it was more with hot-headed rebellion than faith that he encouraged the students to continue with the personalities they had scheduled for the program. Brandon eventually grew hostile and petty in his attitude toward this pastor, and no mutual agreement was ever reached.

God blessed the efforts of the students, but Brandon never tasted peace over that situation. Regardless of whether or not he had been right, Brandon had lost a friend and a supporter. Brandon also lost his earlier enthusiasm for the campus ministry program and eventually for his own faith. He resigned his position and entered another college to study in an altogether different field. It was a year later before Brandon began to understand he had allowed his own ego to destroy his ministry and almost destroy his faith. Eventually, Brandon allowed the light of God's truth to reach him; he realized he had acted on his own strong will and not on God's guidance. Brandon eventually confessed to God the stubborn selfishness of his actions. In doing so, peace and laughter returned to Brandon's heart.

When we let self-will and stubbornness drive us toward achieving our own ends, then it's our ego with which we're concerned and not God. Regardless of how justified we might feel in our opinion, God sees the bigger picture and knows what's best for all concerned, including our decisions. Taking the situation in our own hands and demanding that God justifies our words and actions is actually a rejection of faith in Him. Trusting Him to meet our needs, as well as the needs of those involved, may mean relinquishing our plans and allowing Him to lead us along an unexpected path. Faith is the willingness to travel that path, even when it doesn't seem to meet our desires nor be to our advantage.

SPIRITUAL PREP: 1 Samuel 15:22; 2 Chronicles 30:8; Psalm 95:8; Titus 2:7; 3:2

Getting to Know Myself as a Child of God

Describe your greatest accomplishment:

Living as a Child of God

What do you believe you can do, with God's guidance, to make the world a little better?

PRAYER: Lord Jesus, help me to recognize the difference between stubbornness and faith, between my ego and Your gentle voice. Give me the wisdom and strength to relinquish plans that are not part of Your will.

Exercise 5

· · · · · · · · · · · · · · · ·

LIFETIME STRUGGLE

Have I not commanded you? Be strong and courageous. Do not be afraid;
do not be discouraged, for the Lord your God will be with you wherever you go.
Joshua 1:9

Elizabeth told me about the times she was confident that she had arrived at all of life's answers: when she accepted Christ at age eleven; when a high school friend asked her why she had been mad at her for so long; when she took a religion class in her freshman year of college; when she lost her job, and on and on. With each new situation, whether she successfully encountered it or failed miserably, she kept thinking each new insight gained was the last!

"Ah," Elizabeth thought, "now I understand who I am and what this life is all about. I've finally reached my goal and will be able to handle anything life throws at me. It will be clear skies from now on: no more mistakes, no more misunderstanding on my part." And then, Elizabeth told me, she would run smack into a wall. She would find herself in another troubled relationship or find herself in an unsolvable situation or she'd catch herself seriously doubting God. Mind bruised and head spinning, Elizabeth would wonder how this could have happened. She would find herself once again unsure, less certain of the future, and questioning her faith.

We do not suddenly have all the answers when we become Christians. Mistakes, misunderstandings, and misperceptions continue throughout any lifetime. God promises to be with us in all circumstances. He offers us the clear-mindedness, strength, and compassion to cope—but not necessarily immediate answers. I've frequently been aware of His presence strengthening me and giving me insight into troubled events, and sometimes I've been aware of His intervention in those circumstances. Because of my experiences, however, my faith does not rest well on the expectation that He will make all answers clear or banish all of my problems.

Life remains a struggle for most Christians. It involves the daily effort to understand, to walk wisely, to grow in His will, to love others, to serve Him. I suspect that it's okay, even wise, to recognize that life is often fearful and that our own individual pilgrimage means confronting this fear. When we confront the misunderstandings, failures, hurts, anger, boredom—and yes, joys—we grow. When we acknowledge that no magical power will dissipate all problems nor elevate us beyond their touch, we can learn from them.

We can choose to open our hearts and minds to His guidance in the experiences which make up our reality. We can let the pain or joy of the moment be a winnowing tool, or we can turn from Him because the answers aren't clear. I believe—and have tasted of this myself—that if we consciously choose to rely on God when we face problems, He is with us in His power, in His strength, and in the fullness of His love. He doesn't necessarily provide all the answers on our schedule—and sometimes His answer is "no"—but He will always help us to understand and grow from the problems that we experience. As He manifests His presence to us, somehow we take a step closer to Him in our pilgrimage. In this there is victory. In this there is joy.

SPIRITUAL PREP: 2 Chronicles 15:4; Psalms 9:9; 27:5; 138:7–8, James 1:5

Getting to Know Myself as a Child of God

List some ages and periods in your life when you thought you had found all the answers to life:

List some questions with which you currently struggle:

Living as a Child of God

Spend time in prayer, lifting each of the above questions up to God. Expect God to answer. It may be immediately, tomorrow, or ten years from now when He answers, but He will answer! When He does, record His answer to your questions.

PRAYER: Lord Jesus, when I face problems and have questions, remind me that,
although You may not give me an immediate answer nor alter the circumstances,
You are with me in those circumstances and will help me to find answers.

STEP SEVEN

Living the Christian Life: Prayer

Exercise 1

· · · · · · · · · · · · · · · · ·

PRAYER PROMISES

For no matter how many promises God has made, they are "Yes" in Christ.
And so through him the "Amen" is spoken by us to the glory of God.
2 Corinthians 1:20

I bent down to soothe the small puppy beside the door of the mission church as I arrived to teach Sunday school. It was a freezing winter morning. Ice covered everything, and the little brown pup with huge black eyes stood outside the mission door shivering so hard that he would topple over and have to jump upright again. He begged to go inside to the warmth, so the children and I took him into the trailer and wrapped him in a dry towel for a little while before putting him back outside. But he seemed to have nowhere to go and quickly become covered with the sleeting ice again.

I surveyed the homes in the little village. He belonged to no one. Nor could I impose on the people of this impoverished mountain community to take him into their homes. There was certainly no food to be spared for an animal. The puppy whimpered so mournfully when I once again reached down to brush his fur clean of the ice that I was unable to leave him stranded outside the mission without food or warmth. I took him home with me.

What a bright little animal he was! I named him Laddie. But I was still without a place to keep him. The faculty housing in which I lived wouldn't accept animals and I certainly couldn't move in the dead of winter. Knowing that it was almost impossible to find a home for a stray animal in this town, I decided to ask God for help with the small puppy. "Father," I prayed, "I know this is a very small matter and that there are much more urgent needs in this world, but would You help me find a home for Laddie?"

Within the week, I received a call from a new minister in town. His children had just lost their beloved companion, a collie which had been with the family since the children's birth. He heard about the puppy from a student whom I taught and was wondering if he could adopt it.

Months later, I had the joy of seeing Laddie again. He was almost fully grown, sprawled on the front porch of his new family's home, and encircled by the arms of two very loving children.

The story of Laddie is recorded in the "answered prayer" section of my journal. At the time I wrote it, I was positive that God had taken that situation in His hands. But, typically for me, I didn't sustain the certainty for long. Faced with other problems and needs in my life, I once again began to doubt that He had heard or would answer my prayers.

It has taken me many years to learn to rely, still sometimes reluctantly, on His promises, but as I've come to do so, a change has taken place in my life and work. There is a peace of mind and quiet confidence now regardless of external circumstances. In Him, we truly have an anchor for our lives. It's enough that Christ bore our sins on the cross and that before him we stand totally clean and pure, forgiven, loved, accepted. But there is more. He will meet all our needs and fill the empty places of our hearts. He will respond to our prayers. He will keep His promises.

SPIRITUAL PREP: 1 Kings 8:56; Romans 4:20–21; 2 Corinthians 7:1; Hebrews 10:23; 2 Peter 3:9

Getting to Know Myself as a Child of God

List all the promises that you think of that God has given us:

Describe a time when God specifically answered a prayer promise He made to you:

Living as a Child of God

Describe a prayer you're still waiting for God to answer (and when He does answer it, record the answer here):

PRAYER: Lord, accept my gratitude. Thank you for seeing my needs and meeting
them in ways You know best. You are the anchor of my soul. You are the peace in my life.
You are the joy in my heart. Thank You for being a prayer-answering God.

Exercise 2

. . . .

RECOGNIZING AND AVOIDING MANIPULATION

And when you pray, do not keep on babbling like pagans, for they think they will
be heard because of their many words.
Matthew 6:7

God doesn't apply Band-Aids˚. His is a deep healing process. Many times, in our shortsighted perception of life, we want quick cures and bandages. We pray and pray, and wonder why God doesn't answer our prayers. Perhaps, we think, we've just not made ourselves clear enough about how much we need this thing. Perhaps we just haven't come up with the exact, right words. Somehow, we feel, we must make God aware of the validity and urgency of our request. Then, surely, He'll give us the answer we want.

Prayer isn't a device we use to get our own way. We can't bargain with God, nor is there any magic in saying the right words or repeating a prayer a particular number of times. Even constancy in prayer, while an admirable trait, is not the key to getting our prayers answered. A simple prayer stating our needs and requesting God to fill them is all that is needed.

The parable of the friend who was approached at midnight (Luke 11:5–9) is not told to encourage redundancy in prayer. It's more a parable of contrasts rather than comparison. Instead of making a correlation between the reluctant friend and Christ, it's better for us to view Christ's mercy and receptiveness in contrast to the sleepy resistance of the friend. Unlike the friend, Christ is always ready to hear us, always ready to respond to our petitions. Conversations with the Father are encouraged at all times—not nagging. We can't, as a child might do with a parent, cajole and coax and plead until He gives in to us.

How wonderful to bring our needs and leave them at the feet of Christ. In this we find peace. He hears our heart's longing. He knows us and cares for us. When all else is stripped from us so that our wounds are left bare and cold and all we have is our faith in God, the awesome certainty that he will answer floods our heart and submerges us in the joy of His presence.

SPIRITUAL PREP: Matthew 6:7; Luke 18:11–14; Ephesians 6:17–18

Getting to Know Myself as a Child of God

List five needs that you currently have, in order of importance:

Living as a Child of God

Take some time right now to lift each of the above needs up to God. As He answers each of these needs, keep a record of His answers:

PRAYER: Father, help me to rest in the assurance that You hear all of my prayers, and that you will answer each of them according to Your will. Teach me to not try to manipulate you into doing what I want. Instead, help me to accept Your direction for my life and to walk in obedience to Your guidance.

Exercise 3

· · · · · · · · · · · · · · · · ·

LISTENING IN PRAYER

But when he, the Spirit of truth, comes, he will guide you into all the truth.
He will not speak on his own; he will speak only what he hears,
and he will tell you what is yet to come.
John 16:13

Ginger had just experienced a small taste of victory and wanted to share it with me! After persistent nudging by the Holy Spirit, she finally obeyed His gentle guidance yesterday.

She'd spent hours writing and revising a summary report of her campus ministry activities for the previous month and was ready and eager to send it to her employers. She admitted to me that she didn't exactly have the purest of motivations in writing the report. She wanted those who employed her to be impressed and even awed by all the miraculous progress she'd made. Besides, she was a little put out by a few of those who would receive the report as she felt that they hadn't demonstrated appropriate enthusiasm for what she'd done and for the projects she'd undertaken.

Ginger didn't send the narrative. She wanted to. But the Spirit kept whispering, "No." Even though reasoning urged her to mail it, she backed off from acting on "common sense" and acted, instead, on the still, small, but persistent voice of God.

God frequently uses common sense and good judgment to guide us. Our minds and our intelligence are both gifts from God. We need to develop these gifts as surely as we would develop any gift He bestows. And what a joy it is when God's Spirit affirms our reasoning! What certainty that gives us in our decisions!

However, there are times that the Spirit may counteract even our good, common sense. It takes quietness, strength, humility, and a listening ear ever tuned to God to hear the heartfelt voice of His Spirit. After more than forty years, Ginger admitted she was only beginning to learn to discern it. In addition to her own natural stubbornness, Ginger was not exposed to those who spoke much of the Holy Spirit until her adult years. She told me that it was almost as if He were a family member about whom she wasn't allowed to talk. He was there, but it seemed He must not be permitted to come out into the open too often. Ginger was led to believe that people might get the wrong impression of the family if she spoke of the joy of the Spirit too frequently or too eagerly acknowledged His role in her life. Heaven help her if she ever raised her hands in worship, sang too exuberantly, or clapped in the sheer joy of His presence. People might get the wrong idea!

It was almost presented as a choice she was forced to make: between being an intelligent, thinking, stable person, or a person who expressed the joy of being filled with the Holy Spirit. I agreed with Ginger that churches who stifle the movement of the Spirit are missing a great deal! What a delight it is to find an intelligent individual who opens her life to the Holy Spirit without fear of people's reactions to the manifestation of God's Spirit in her thoughts, words, and actions.

Many times, Ginger admits she still goes her own way, ignoring the gentle nudging of the Holy Spirit, until disaster sets in. But when she does listen . . . oh, the joy, the triumph, the *rightness* of it. To our Creator every decision that we make is important, large or small, and His Spirit is with us to guide us into all truth as we take the time to listen.

SPIRITUAL PREP: Proverbs 1:33; Isaiah 55:3; Jeremiah 33:3; John 14:16–17

Getting to Know Myself as a Child of God

Describe a time when the Holy Spirit nudged you to take a specific path. What was the outcome? What did the Spirit teach you, as a result?

Living as a Child of God

Think quietly for a few moments about the areas of your life where you depend upon the guidance of the Holy Spirit. Describe them below.

Where do you sense the Spirit calling you to depend more upon Him now? What do you think that would look like? Write your thoughts below.

PRAYER: Father, what joy the presence of Your Holy Spirit brings to my life! Help me to listen, to be sensitive to His guidance, and to rejoice in whatever direction He leads.

Exercise 4

· · · · · · · · · · · · · · · · ·

REVELATION THROUGH PRAYER

As the deer pants for streams of water, so my soul pants for you, my God.
My soul thirsts for God, for the living God.
Psalm 42:1–2a

Once I read a short novel about a young widow who chose to join a charity group. This woman later became a martyr for her faith. Touched and inspired by the story, I wanted to give my heart to God in the same pure and total way demonstrated by this young woman. How I wished for the qualities of this widow. My motive was sincere. The glory of being a martyr was not my desire, but the longing for her dedication and singular love of God was overwhelming.

In moments of disclosure, God sometimes speaks so directly that the impact of His presence leaves us stunned. Such an incident—small, but revealing—happened soon after this. My desire to live as this young woman had not been an urgent prayer request, although it had been a sincere one. Perhaps it was the insignificant nature of these circumstances that sharpened the clarity of His response to me. Despite the brevity of the book, the impression made by its story stayed with me.

Two days after finishing the book, with the longing still fresh and undiminished in my heart, I began my regular morning devotions. The reading that morning was about the same young widow portrayed in the book. Instantly, I knew: God had heard my heart's desire. The impact and clarity of His response was intense. I was almost blinded for a moment to the rest of the reading while I sat, as it were, face to face with God. My soul thirsted for Him as it never had before, and my heart literally sang His praise. It really didn't matter what the rest of the reading said. I knew God cared. I knew He was with me and was listening to my every thought. Without a doubt, I knew He was letting me know that He had heard my heart's desire and that He approved.

How beautiful to realize that God walks this close to us, that He will communicate so clearly. I realized that any sincere desire to be more like Him, more the person He created us to be, will be heard and answered. But oh, the joy of knowing that He will speak with such directness! He will hear our cry to be His servants, to love him, and to obey Him. He will point the way, strengthen us, and commune with us as we travel with Him, side by side.

SPIRITUAL PREP: Psalm 33:9; Isaiah 58:9a; Luke 12:12; 1 Corinthians 2:10–13

Getting to Know Myself as a Child of God

When has God's presence or His will for your life been made especially clear to you? Describe it below.

Living as a Child of God

How have those occurrences changed the trajectory of your life? Your perceptions of who God is?

PRAYER: Jesus, how wonderful is Your companionship. How marvelous it is when I can hear Your voice so clearly! Thank You for reminding me that You're personally involved in my life.

Exercise 5

· · · · · · · · · · · · · · · · · ·

A LIFELINE OF PRAYER

He gives strength to the weary and increases the power of the weak.
Isaiah 40:29

The movie focused on the fireman as he threw a rope to the young teenage boy. The adolescent secured the rope on something in the dark, smoke-filled room and clambered down to safety. As I watched this remarkable rescue, I thought, "How like that rope prayer can be."

Prayer is the lifeline provided by God for each of us. When we're weary and feel like we're facing impossible odds, when the fires of our lives threaten to overwhelm us: that's when we most need to grab of Him in prayer. He is our Source of strength. Each of us has weaknesses we cannot conquer and problems we cannot solve except by reaching out to this higher source of strength through prayer.

Sometimes the weight of the world—the pressures, the deadlines, and the expectations placed on us—so crowd us that it's difficult to make the time to spend alone with God, and because of that our hands slip from the very lifeline we need. We reach a point where we feel so tired, exhausted, and dismal that life becomes an unwanted burden rather than an exciting pilgrimage spent learning about and growing in Christ. We use up all our energy and spend all our time fighting the fires of the world, leaving us discouraged and disinclined to spend time with Him. We give up the very lifeline we need most.

Too often, it's only after I've become exhausted with my own efforts that I finally turn to look into God's face to ask Him what's happening—only to see the lifeline God has been waiting to throw me all along. At these moments, I realize that it was because I had depended so much on my own pathetic strength that I exhausted myself. Without going to Him in prayer, seeking His will, I had rushed to put out the blaze of fire and found my eyes filled with smoke and my lungs gasping for a clean breath of air.

When I was a child, prayer was telling God what I wanted or needed Him to do for me. As I matured, I learned that prayer is so much more. Prayer is our pathway not only to divine protection, but also to a personal, intimate relationship with God. Prayer is more than asking, it requires listening as well. Being still, quiet, and waiting for God to speak is a key to the power of prayer. I believe that during difficult times God provides a special lifeline woven of love, strength, and healing which we can access through prayer. And if we make an effort to lift our eyes to Him—no matter how dire our circumstances—we'll find that he holds out this rope of life for us.

No matter what's happening to us—whether we're experiencing the fires of disease, pain, loss, failure—we have a tool on our side that changes everything: prayer. God does seem, so often, to choose the weak and helpless through whom to do His mighty works. Perhaps it's because in these individuals there can be no vaunting of human effort—only a simple, upward cry of need toward which He can cast His lifeline of love.

SPIRITUAL PREP: Psalms 34:17; 50:15; 55:16–18; 86:5–7; 91:15–16

Getting to Know Myself as a Child of God

Describe a time when you needed God to throw you a lifeline.
Were you aware of it at the time? If so, what did it involve? Describe it below:

Living as a Child of God

In what situations do you need God to throw you a lifeline now? What might that look like?

PRAYER: My energy is exhausted, and I am so tired from doing things in my own strength.
Remind me, Father, that You are waiting to throw a lifeline to me. Teach me to trust You completely.

Living the Christian Life: Witnessing

Exercise 1

. . . .

OUR MOTIVATION FOR WITNESSING

"You are my witnesses," declares the Lord, "and my servant whom I have chosen,
so that you may know and believe me and understand that I am he."
Isaiah 43:10

There is not a single individual whom God wants left out of His redemptive plan for mankind. Every person is a creation of God, and He longs after each person as any parent would long after his child. As Christians, we are a unique source of introduction to this heavenly Father Who died on the cross for our sins. But what does it mean to be a "witness"? And how do we go about this task of witnessing?

You don't need training to become a witness. You've probably been witnessing for years, perhaps without even realizing it, by the type of life you lead. You may not be aware of all the people who have been watching and learning from you, but you are already a witness to something. The question is, to what have you been witnessing? What do people see when they're watching you? Do they see somebody who has seen and heard and felt the power of Jesus Christ?

I've encountered a few Christians who've felt that witnessing meant that they must convert others to their particular set of doctrines, believing that new converts could not possibly belong to the family of God otherwise. These witnesses seemed more concerned with chalking up the numbers, convinced of their perception of the Christian experience, than with sharing Christ's love. In some cases, it has almost seemed as if they had a compulsive need to impose their own yokes onto the shoulders of new converts. I suspect that this need to convince others of the validity of their doctrines and burdens reflects their own self-doubts about the rituals they try so hard to follow.

You may not have all the methods and booklets and angles in your grasp; you may not even know all the doctrines of the Bible. But if you've been walking with Jesus Christ, you've got something to say. What's more, you're never alone in this. The Holy Spirit has been sent into the world to bear witness to Christ, and the Holy Spirit is in you. You can be a firsthand living testimony to Jesus Christ through the power of the Holy Spirit. When you know Jesus Christ—when you have heard Him and when He has touched your life—you become one who can tell about Him. That is far more important than knowing doctrines or formulas.

Once you've shared the love that Christ demonstrated on the cross, leave it up to the Holy Spirit to do the convincing. Jesus did not call us to impose our personal yokes and doctrines on others, but to introduce others to Him. He called us to the joy and freedom of sharing His love, out of the wellspring of our relationship with Him.

As we draw nearer to God, our yokes assume less importance. Instead, we desire that God becomes everything to every person. The peace that we experience in our walk with Christ is the peace we want for everyone. We wish to share the joy and confidence that accompanies His presence abiding with us. His compassion and concern for all mankind becomes our concern. Out of that concern, we desire to tell others the wonderful news of Christ's death on the cross for the forgiveness of our sins.

SPIRITUAL PREP: Psalms 119:171–172; 145:2–7; Isaiah 44:8; Matthew 5:16; Acts 26:16

Getting to Know Myself as a Child of God

In the following space, write your testimony of how you came to accept Christ and what this has meant for your life. Include the time, place, circumstances, and persons involved. Use extra paper as needed.

Living as a Child of God

Rehearse sharing your testimony a few times. Then, ask some Christian friends to listen as you share your testimony with them. Continue practicing until you feel completely comfortable sharing your testimony. Ask God to provide opportunities for you to share your testimony with others—and begin looking out for the opportunities, trusting that God will answer your prayer.

PRAYER: God, keep me ever mindful of the difference between man's traditions and Your truth. Make my concern to be to share Your love with others, not to make them live the Christian life as I live or view it.

Exercise 2

· · · · · · · · · · · · · · · · ·

PREPARATION FOR WITNESSING

Now that you have purified yourselves by obeying the truth so that you have sincere love for each other, love one another deeply, from the heart.
1 Peter 1:22

My grandmother (on my father's side) lived in an old two-story, rough-hewed plank home in the backwoods of North Carolina. Nothing extravagant, it was a nice house adequate for the seven children raised in it. A wooden porch surrounded the house. Next to the back door always sat a large, sparkling clean tin bucket.

I can remember many hot summer afternoons spent playing in the yard behind that house. Sweaty and tired after a day of "hide-n'-seek" or "cowboys-n'-Indians," we would rush to the bucket, and with the shiny silver dipper hanging beside it, scoop out some of the freshest, sweetest, coolest water you've ever tasted. My grandmother always made certain that the bucket was filled to the brim with water so we could enjoy its cool refreshment.

In the same way, I have found that I need to be "filled" with God's love before I can share it with others. Every day with a cup of hot tea, and with my Bible and journal in hand, I sit facing the window as the sun's first warming rays creep like soft fingers into the dark coolness of the early morning sky. I enjoy spending the first hour of each day with God, when my thoughts are clearest and my needs most apparent. My mind is more receptive to whatever material I read during that first, fresh hour of each new day, and retains it longer. I want the content of that material to be conversations between God and I.

It's during these precious morning times that I ask God to warm my heart with His presence and cleanse me from sin. It's during this time, before I become lost in the business of the day, that I read His Word. I'm most aware of and comforted by His Holy Spirit in the morning without whom my witness would be meaningless. Only by the work of His Spirit through me will others be drawn to Him. Only by the work of the Holy Spirit will words and programs, inspired by Him, take hold and meet the needs of a hurting world.

As I allow myself to be guided by God's Spirit throughout my day, I often find myself reminding students that, even though I am willing to work with them, their best counselor is God. Certainly no one knows the mind of each person better than God. He is the source of all life; He is the great healer. When I counsel, I recognize that I must allow His love and His truth to reach through my stumbling efforts to heal this troubled person.

The tools of my trade are of little value apart from Him. While He may use my hands and my words, it is still God, through Christ, who soothes the troubled heart and brings peace out of wilted dreams. He will reach into past hurts to bind old wounds and forgive errant ways. I can only serve as the facilitator who helps others to rise above their life circumstances and come to rest at the feet of Christ. Having spent the morning hours in His presence, I'm more able to direct others to their true Source of help.

SPIRITUAL PREP: Joshua 1:8; Lamentations 3:22–23; Acts 1:8; 1 Timothy 4:15–16

Getting to Know Myself as a Child of God

Write out a schedule for your complete day below. Include a time for devotions in your schedule.

Living as a Child of God

List the materials that you currently use and/or will need for your devotional times (i.e., notebook, pen, Bible, devotional magazines, books, etc.). Then gather those items in a spot that is quiet and private, where you will meet God each day at the time specified in your schedule:

PRAYER: Lord Jesus, help me to set aside time each day to spend with You, and to remain faithful to keeping that time. During these quiet moments, fill my heart to the brim with Your love so that I can't help but let it spill over in witness about You.

Exercise 3

· · · · · · · · · · · · · · · ·

THE OFFENSIVE WITNESS

When pride comes, then comes disgrace; but with humility comes wisdom.
Proverbs 11:2

Early in my college teaching career, I encountered Luke. When first meeting him, Luke was not unpleasant to be around, but he seemed to eventually alienate almost everyone with whom he came in contact. His approach to sharing the good news of Christ was abrasive. The gospel seemed like a weapon wielded against others for whom he held the utmost contempt. Witnessing appeared to be a means of demonstrating his superiority over lesser persons.

And perhaps he needed this weapon. Luke's mother had died shortly after his birth, and he had been abandoned by his father. I found myself wishing that he would seek counseling, and even attempted to gently suggest this to him. However, his pride left no room for admission of such a need. Nor did it leave time for him to admit the need to study in order to complete his college classes.

Slowly, but clearly, Luke was destroying his own opportunities to minister for Christ. His grades dropped. He not only got himself blocked from visitation rights at the local hospital and juvenile home, but his reputation caused the doors to be barred against other students from the college who wished to do visitation. His pride—a protection from his own feelings of insecurity and fear of failure—was disgracing him and bringing ill repute on other Christians associated with him.

I believe that Luke longed to be called a friend and a child of God. I remain hopeful that he will achieve this reputation in his lifetime. But at the time I knew him, his unresolved problems dominated his personality. Someday, perhaps, when he's willing to face those problems and come to grips with his fear and insecurity, when he faces his anger at those who abandoned him, God will take the hurt and the potential for growth and turn Luke into a truly mighty witness for Him.

How do people respond to your witness? If they reject your testimony, be slow to assume that it's because the people to whom you're witnessing are obstinate and not ready to hear. Take time to examine yourself before God. Allow Him to show you if there's a need to change the way you witness about His love.

SPIRITUAL PREP: Romans 16:17–18; Galatians 5:22–23; 1 Thessalonians 3:11–12; Hebrews 10:24

Getting to Know Myself as a Child of God

Describe some situations in which you'd like to be able to witness:

Tell how you would feel most comfortable witnessing in those situations:

Living as a Child of God

Now, spend some time in prayer, lifting up each of the situations in which you'd like to witness and asking God to give you the opportunities and courage to do so.

PRAYER: Lord Jesus, as I examine how I witness, shed Your light on any need I might have to change my style or attitude. Help me to always witness in respect, love, and compassion for the other person's feelings.

Exercise 4

· · · · · · · · · · · · · · · · · ·

FINDING THE WORDS

He then said to me: "Son of man, go now to the people of Israel
and speak my words to them."
Ezekiel 3:4

Beth grew up without knowing that her lifetime friend, Sandra, was a Christian. When Beth became a Christian as an adult, she was eager to tell Sandra about her new faith. When she called with the news, she learned that Sandra had been a Christian for many years but had never talked about it with Beth until this moment. So much heartache in Beth's life might have been avoided if only Sandra had shared her Christian beliefs.

When we hear about something really new and exciting, catch it on TV, or read about it on Facebook, we can't wait to share it. We're eager to tell our friends and close acquaintances and, if the news is good enough, we even want strangers to benefit from it.

God's forgiving, redemptive love offered to us through Christ's death on the cross is the best news anyone will ever hear. Our world is a hurting place and, wherever we are, people are desperate for forgiveness and healing in their lives. As Christians, we hold in our hands the secret of that forgiveness and healing. We have experienced the joy of being adopted into God's family, and the peace and happiness which He provides is sufficient and full and will spill over to those around us—if we let it.

Your circumstances provide you with your mission field. There are so many who have heard only a partial or distorted version of the truth. While it's probably accurate to say that the most observable and consistent witness you can offer is your behavior and lifestyle, there are times when you'll need to openly speak about His role in your life. A natural and comfortable acknowledgment of God's love, through the guidance of His Holy Spirit, is all that's needed.

The mature Christian lifestyle is so filled with His Spirit that we long to share His joy with those with whom we live, work, and play. How fulfilling to be so intimately involved with our Heavenly Father that we have no fear of speaking His name nor revealing our relationship with Him. How marvelous and exciting to know that He is using our actions and our words to attract others to the Christ whose Spirit dwells within us.

SPIRITUAL PREP: Exodus 4:11–12; Psalm 35:28; Ecclesiastes 3:7; Luke 12:12 Acts 18:9–10

Getting to Know Myself as a Child of God

List ten people with whom you'd like to share the good news of Jesus:

Living as a Child of God

In the space above, next to their names, write what you'd like to say to each of the ten people you just listed.

PRAYER: Lord Jesus, nudge my heart when a verbal witness is appropriate.
Put the words in my mouth that will draw others close to you.

Exercise 5

• • • • • • • • • • • • • • • •

WINNING THE BATTLE

If anyone will not welcome you or listen to your words,
leave that home or town and shake the dust off your feet."
Matthew 10:14

Have you ever thought that you were fighting a losing battle? It seems like a bitter failure when we have to give up on convincing a resisting heart and mind of the truth of God. Sometimes we react personally, as though it were a threat to our own pride, when the other person doesn't accept what we're trying to tell them. We've been caring about and praying for this soul for days, weeks, even months; still he or she remains untouched by our earnest attempts to show them God's love. Or, we've spent hours trying to motivate enthusiasm for a ministry that we're certain will draw hundreds of people to Christ, but no one else seems interested.

For forty years Moses felt like a "has-been," a criminal, and a failure. He had killed a man in a burst of anger and had fled from his own country. His royal upbringing seemed wasted; now he faced middle age away from his own people and his own land. Even when God offered him a tremendous opportunity, Moses held back, made excuses, and begged for compromise. The task seemed too large for him.

When we encounter resistance to our efforts to let others know the story of Christ, our reactions are often like those of Moses. We pull back. The task seems too large for us. We make excuses and beg for compromise. We point to those who appear more capable and holy, and decide that Christ's Great Commission is best meant for them, not us.

If we were left with only the Great Commission to spread the good news, or if it were left up to our devices to become holy enough to witness, then there would be an authentic reason for despair. However, the same God who calls us also enables us. By simple faith in Christ—by putting our hand in His and giving our lives to Him—He will strengthen us, fill us with His Spirit, and guide us as we attempt to witness for Him.

Certainly you'll feel some sadness when it appears that the working of the Holy Spirit is blocked. You may mourn the tragic loss of God's truth for the individual who refuses to accept it. But remember: that person, that program, is in God's hands. Take up His rod of truth and continue to seek your place of service. Leave the results with God.

SPIRITUAL PREP: 1 Samuel 17:47; 2 Chronicles 20:15; 2 Corinthians 2:14–15; Galatians 6:9

Getting to Know Myself as a Child of God

Describe a situation in which you tried to be a witness but was rejected

How did this make you feel?

Living as a Child of God

Spend a few minutes talking with the Lord about the rejection of your witness. Ask Him if He would have had you do anything differently. Record His response to you below (and if it was to confirm the way you witnessed, write down that confirmation).

PRAYER: Father, once You've given me the courage to witness,
help me not to take the results personally. Remind me often that, although I may be
the one who is witnessing, it is the Holy Spirit who draws others to You.

Living the Christian Life: Purpose

Exercise 1

· · · · · · · · · · · · · · · ·

INTERPRETING OUR CALL

Now to him who is able to do immeasurably more than all we ask or imagine . . .
Ephesians 3:20

"Pat, this is Pastor Jim. I was wondering if you'd play the piano for our nursing home ministry. We're pretty desperate for someone to play."

"You *must* be desperate if you want to subject them to my piano playing," I laughed. Among any talents I have, music is the least developed. But I enjoy playing the piano, even though my hearing impairment limits my ability to master the skill. So I began to play for the nursing home ministry.

What dear hearts the residents were! Never once did they complain about my frequent wrong notes; they just loved to sing! And I found the weekly hour at the nursing home to be one of the highlights of my week.

"It's not your abilities that God wants but your availability," declares a popular poster. We're all called to be His ministers. Whether a student, housewife, professional, retired person, missionary, or church pastor, it's not the skills on which we pride ourselves that matter; it's our availability to Him.

Through our walk with Jesus Christ, we flower into people with all the beauty with which God imbued us. God made us, and He created all that which is lovely in our being. Only He can bring to fruition all He means for us to be . The world certainly won't. The world will lead us down a path that inhibits, distorts, and destroys that which is good in us. But as we make our lives available to God, we may find ourselves caught by surprise at the talents He brings out in us and the opportunities He gives us to use them.

What can you give Him? An arm around a child's shoulder? A strong voice for reading stories? Skills to lead a Bible study? All of us can do something for Jesus. Leaning on Him, the Author of all truth and beauty, He will encourage our hearts and minds and show us how to use that which is best in each of us. As we make ourselves available to God, our talents will take shape. With His guidance, we can live and work and love so that He is glorified.

SPIRITUAL PREP: Psalm 32:8–9; Proverbs 3:5–6; Galatians 6:10, Ephesians 4:1–3; 1 Peter 1:15–16

Getting to Know Myself as a Child of God

Special talents the Lord has given me:

Talents that I wish I had:

Living as a Child of God

Describe three ways you'd like to serve God, and identify the talents you'd need to do so:

PRAYER: Father God, help me to identify my talents and use my abilities to Your glory! It is delightful to see my skills, however slight, used in Your service.

Exercise 2

· · · · · · · · · · · · · · · · ·

USING OUR TALENTS

The LORD is my strength and my shield; my heart trusts in him, and he helps me.
My heart leaps for joy, and with my song I praise him.
Psalm 28:7

My friend Bruce has a great tenor voice. It's the best I've ever heard. Yet, every effort by Bruce to use his talent has run into impossible barriers. Bruce made a CD, but it didn't sell. Still, my friend continues to train and to sing whenever the opportunity presents itself.

I can listen to Bruce sing and know that he's praising God with his whole heart; his voice seems to float on angels' wings. How God must stop and listen with a smile on His face and with eyes shining with love each time Bruce sings. God will use that talent. Neither I nor my friend knows how or when. But that doesn't matter; Bruce continues to sing.

Ronald Dunn, in his book *When Heaven Is Silent*, makes a very good point: when your efforts are blocked or you face a particularly difficult barrier, instead of asking "Why?" ask "What now?" The "why" may never be answered, but the "what now" takes our eyes off the past and gives us a future, a hope. It expresses our faith that God has our best interests in mind.

Have your efforts to use your skills and talents been rebuffed or ignored? Have you begun to doubt that you have any special abilities and given up on using the gifts you once thought were yours? Do you think about hiding what you've been able to accomplish and ceased to practice the skills He's given you because you see no earthly way they can be used? No matter how discouraged you might be, don't give up. Continue to develop these talents. Discipline yourself. Trust Him to take the product of your effort and use it to His glory. Find your own individual race and run it for Him. Then, when you lay down to rest at night, you'll do so with the peace that comes from knowing you've done all you can to use your God-given abilities.

You can wake in the morning with praise on your lips and a song to Him in your heart. Work on making your skills the best they can be; let your thoughts dwell on Him as you exercise your talents; allow yourself to experience the joy of knowing you're doing your best for Him. Have confidence that because you've obeyed, He will bless your efforts. In Him, you do have a future and a hope.

SPIRITUAL PREP: Psalm 1:3; Romans 12:6–8; 1 Corinthians 12:4–6; 1 Timothy 4:14

Getting to Know Myself as a Child of God

My dream for this world is:

Living as a Child of God

How can you use your talents to help make this dream come true?

PRAYER: Father, fill my heart with the peace of knowing that I've done my best to develop and exercise my gifts. Assure me that You will use my efforts, although I may not see how at this moment.

Exercise 3

· · · · · · · · · · · · · · · ·

SERVING WHERE?

Also, seek the peace and prosperity of the city to which I have carried you into exile.
Pray to the LORD for it, because if it prospers, you too will prosper.
Jeremiah 29:7

It was a particularly pleasant summer afternoon. The sun was bright and there was a cool breeze outside, so I left the door to my garden apartment opened as I worked. I had spent the earlier hours of the day hanging wallpaper in the kitchen of my new faculty housing and getting to know some of the neighbors who dropped by to chat and hang wallpaper along with me. Later, I was able to catch up on correspondence that had been weeks behind, and then attend evening services at church.

I felt good about being in this place. Although I was now in the western part of the country, far away from my longtime home on the East Coast, it felt right being here. A cocoon-like warmth surrounded me. I knew that I was in God's will. I was optimistic about teaching. It was and still is my favorite work, but I no longer wore the rose-colored glasses of my youth's ambition. I realized that here, too, there would be difficult times.

And so it has been in all of the places to which He has called me to serve—both the joy-filled days and those filled with difficult times. I've known the warm fellowship of working alongside giants in the Christian faith while, at the same time, having to cooperate with those who plotted and schemed to hold on to positions which demanded skills different from their own. I've seen the reputation of many colleagues muddled by jealousy, gossip, and half-truths. I've faced the contradiction of having a job well-done ignored or perceived as a threat rather than encouraged. I've felt the frustration of having integrity interpreted as disloyalty and responsibility seen as a lack of cooperation. But by God's grace, the difficulties in these places of service became opportunities to exercise faith. And the kinder, gentler folks became my people, my family.

Have you been apportioned a rocky, stern place to scatter seed? As God's servant, do you sow on unyielding ground? Don't despair, and don't doubt your call. Finish the task He has given you. If God has you in this place, there may be lessons for you to learn as well as service rendered which will draw you into a closer walk with Him. Lean heavily on Him. Search for His strength and His wisdom. He'll show you the way over the boulders that cause you to stumble and bruise your sore feet. He is with you in your place of service and He will not forsake you. And when it comes time to leave, He'll gently nudge your heart and show you the door to service elsewhere so that you'll have no doubt about His direction for you.

SPIRITUAL PREP: Isaiah 6:8; Jonah 3:1–3; Matthew 24:14; 28:19–20; 1 Corinthians 16:9

Getting to Know Myself as a Child of God

Describe a difficult circumstance in which you tried to serve God or would have liked to serve Him. What was the outcome of your efforts?

Living Life as a Child of God

Where and how would you like to serve God in the future? What obstacles do you anticipate as you try to move into this area of service?

PRAYER: Father, if I'm ever in a difficult place and things aren't going as I'd hoped,
help me to continue to serve You and to draw the support I need from Your abiding presence.
Show me how to feel at home wherever You send me.

Exercise 4

· · · · · · · · · · · · · · · · ·

SERVICE, OR AMBITION?

My heart, O God, is steadfast; I will sing and make music with all my soul. Awake, harp
and lyre! I will awaken the dawn.
Psalm 108:1–2

I can't slow down. There's too many things that people expect me to do!" Monica exclaimed as she bemoaned her health problems. Her doctor warned her that her heart condition was stress-related, but she was unwilling to make the changes in her lifestyle that would enable her to recover. Monica constantly complained about what was expected of her as if she had no choice but to comply.

Have you met someone like this? They insist that they've no time to enjoy the leisurely things in life because they're so busy with church activities, family expectations, employer demands, and doing things for other people. They wring their hands and furrow their brows and rush rapidly about to get all the things done that they feel only they can do. They develop stomach trouble and high blood pressure and yet accelerate the pace of their "ministry." It appears that their feelings of worth stem from how busy and overworked they are.

God doesn't ask us to maintain a pace that's self-destructive. He created us to spend long moments of relaxed communion and heart-lifting worship with Him. He made a world so full of autumn beauty and spring perfume that, even alone, a lifetime could be spent in quiet, unhurried enjoyment and praise. He does not ask us to make ourselves useful to Him; He asks us to surrender our strong will so that He can use us. If we give Him the reins of our lives, He will put in our hearts melodies to write and gentle songs to sing and will call us to calm moments of soul-lifting liturgy.

Our Lord does not need our busyness to get His work accomplished. He merely offers us the opportunity to enjoy His world and work with Him as He leads in His plan of redemption for mankind. He can do nicely without our help, but nonetheless calls us into service out of His great love and concern for us. Far more important than any busy work we do is the time we spend in sweet communion with God. That communion itself—not what we accomplish by our own efforts—is what will make our time on earth meaningful.

SPIRITUAL PREP: Psalms 23:1–2; 46:10; Luke 10:38–42; 1 Thessalonians 4:9–12

Getting to Know Myself as a Child of God

Describe a time when you became so busy that you felt overwhelmed. What was your part in becoming overwhelmed?

Living as a Child of God

Think again about that time you felt overwhelmed. Describe how you might have slowed down and used your time more effectively:

PRAYER: Lord Jesus, quiet my hurrying heart and calm my busy mind
so that I may always be sensitive to your sweet Spirit.

Exercise 5

. . . .

DOUBTING OUR SERVICE

He called out to them, "Friends, haven't you any fish?" "No," they answered. He said,
"Throw your net on the right side of the boat and you will find some."
John 21:5–6

Leon could see no real accomplishments from his previous four years as a campus minister. He had resigned from that position and was now employed as an assistant professor of history in a different university. Since there wasn't a program of campus ministry at his new place of employment, he'd volunteered, while serving as a professor, to try and start one. He had hoped the program would involve the students in student-led Bible studies, missions, and community service; however, he encountered the very same resistance to voluntary participation in the program as he had during his tenure as a full-time campus minister.

A dull cloud of doubt began to settle about Leon as he questioned himself and God. God had brought him to this place and given him these sheep to take care of, hadn't He? Why then did he always feel like such a miserable failure? Everything he touched seemed to go wrong. Leon was certain that all of his efforts had failed. He could see no response on the part of the students to his teaching or attempts to foster a campus ministry program.

As Leon strolled across the campus grounds one day, he was met by one of his fellow faculty members who had a favor to ask of Leon. The students had selected Leon as one of their favorite teachers and wanted to know if he would take part on a panel to share how he related to students.

Little did this faculty member know how much Leon felt the touch of God's hand as he was told this exciting news. Here Leon had thought that his efforts to share God's love with his students had fallen on deaf ears; even more, he'd begun to doubt that God had any part in calling him to this place. All the while, God had been using Leon and had been gathering fish in a quantity he never would have imagined possible. While Leon had been bemoaning his fate, God had been working.

The power of God who loves sin-stained persons—the power of God who brings the winter storms and the new spring rains—the power of God who died on the cross for us and then rose again from the dead— the power of that God can take our frail efforts and, through them, accomplish miracles. He *will* work miracles and reach others through you as you make an effort to serve Him.

SPIRITUAL PREP: Isaiah 46:11; Philippians 4:13; Hebrews 10:23; 2 Peter 3:9

Getting to Know Myself as a Child of God

Describe a time when you tried to serve God but thought you had failed:

Living as a Child of God

Looking back at that time, describe how God might have used you in that situation despite what you thought—or what God *has* revealed to you since that time:

PRAYER: God, help me know You're at work through me, even when I cannot see.
Strengthen my faith until it is as steady as the touch of Your hand.

Exercise 6

· · · · · · · · · · · · · · · ·

HUMILITY IN SERVICE

I have become a sign to many; you are my strong refuge.
Psalm 71:7

After Sue had graduated from our college, she'd accepted a position as an assistant to the dean of women. She was looking forward to her first trip to a national conference for college deans with awe for the reputations of some of the respected professionals whom she'd meet at the national conference. Several of them were even legendary. Relatively new in the field, she was certain that everyone would notice how green behind the ears she was.

At the conference, Sue found the participating professionals to be as charming and interesting as she'd imagined. Because of her own shyness in social situations, however, she tended to pull away to some isolated corner in the crowded hall, especially when many of those attending were justifiably relating accomplishments in their particular place of work. It took Sue completely unaware when one dean, well known in the field, approached her rather breathlessly and said, "I've been trying to find out where you were because I've heard so much about you."

Sue told me that the surprise must have registered on her face, as she managed to sputter some meaningless garble of appreciation for the compliment and struggled to look professional and worthy of the remark. Sue laughed as she related that her ego, in those few, short seconds, expanded rather remarkably. Almost instantly, Sue said, she began to see herself as outstanding, perhaps destined to be a better college dean than most. Her youth and lack of experience was forgotten. She must have been doing pretty miraculous things, she thought, for news of her work to have reached the ears of the outstanding elderly dean!

Pride, power, and greed are triplets. When pride takes over, we forget that the Source of all which is good and productive in us is God. Pride tells us that we are somehow better equipped than others intellectually, socially, and/or spiritually. Pride leads us to feel powerful, and we become greedy for recognition and more power over other lives. When we become proud, we allow ourselves to be consumed with our own resourcefulness and expect acknowledgment of our superiority from others.

It was later in the evening, Sue said, when she returned to her hotel room, shut out the social clatter, and turned quietly to an evening devotion that reality set in. Certainly, she possessed skills and talents of a sort, but these were gifts from God and had become fruitful only under His guidance. It was only as Sue trusted God with her life, releasing every effort on her part, that God had made Sue's work to shine with His glory.

Sue was deeply grateful that God had let her know that He had used her work and that Sue was, indeed, special to Him. In the quietness of the moment Sue recognized that God was her strong refuge and that her singular desire became once again to serve Him. Knowing Him, Sue said, surpassed anything that puffed-up pride, power, or recognition could offer. God was Sue's peace, Sue's joy—and, through her all-too-human body and mind, Sue's success. He will be your success also, as you recognize and give credit to His miraculous touch in your efforts to serve Him.

SPIRITUAL PREP: Psalms 9:12; 131; Proverbs 18:12; Micah 6:8; Acts 20:18–24; Galatians 6:14

Getting to Know Myself as a Child of God

Earlier in this book, humility was described as letting go of your circumstances and leaving them in God's hands, trusting Him to take care of you. Describe some circumstances of which you need to let go and leave in God's hands right now:

Describe how you feel about leaving these circumstances in God's hands:

Living as a Child of God

Over time, watch for God to work in the circumstances described above. As you see what He does, record it here:

PRAYER: Lord Jesus, thank You for letting me know that I am special to You,
and that you have given me unique talents and skills. Keep me mindful that I exercise
my talents best when I look to You and allow You to work through me.

STEP TEN

Living the Christian Life Victoriously

Exercise 1

. . . .

THE RETURN OF SPRING

This is the day which the Lord has made; let us rejoice and be glad in it.
Psalm 118:24 (RSV)

Spring has returned. A neighbor has just brought me a handful of her garden's daffodils. The cats are begging to go outside to chase the returning robins, and windows are stripped of their winter glass to admit the soft, warm breeze. At the college, the students restlessly daydream away class lectures or loll in pairs and small groups on the campus grass. This is indeed a glorious day which the Lord has made, and it's easy to rejoice and be glad in it.

But what about the days when there are no fresh, spring breezes or warm sunshine, when there are no bright yellow daffodils or romantic thoughts about which to daydream? Did the Lord design these days also? Where is the cause for rejoicing and for being glad in them? During the long periods when the skies have been overcast for weeks and each day passes without any vision of green grass or new romance, where do we look to find evidence of His presence and feel the gentle touch of His love?

Perhaps the necessity for these days is in teaching us that the place to find Him is not only in the natural world around us, even with its breathtaking beauty, but in our walk, day by day, and minute by minute in His presence.

Even the dreariest of days can be warmed by the presence of God's Spirit and by the grasp of His hand as we walk through the circumstances that crowd our lives. He is always with us, in drab days as well as bright ones. We only need to recognize His presence to grasp hope and joy again. There's nothing that man or nature can do to rob us of this joy. No one can take the eternal springtime from our hearts when they are filled with His love.

SPIRITUAL PREP: Esther 9:21–22; Psalms 42:11; 126:5–6; Isaiah 55:12; Jeremiah 31:13

I Am a Child of God!

Congratulations! You've worked hard, and have already come a long way in finding and expressing the person God wants you to be!

1. If you could live anywhere in the world you wanted to live, where would it be?

2. If you could be an expert in any subject, what would it be?

3. What would you do if you knew you could not fail?

Also be sure to study your photo as you finish each of the last three exercises of this book, and spend time praising God for making you the gifted, talented person you are.

PRAYER: Jesus, even in the darkest of days, keep Your eternal springtime alive in my heart.

Exercise 2

• • • • • • • • • • • • • • • •

A WARM FIRE, A NEW FRIEND, AND A PLOT OF EARTH

When the Lord saw her, his heart went out to her and he said, "Don't cry."

Luke 7:13

A book was loaned to me not too many months ago. The author, a Christian, had won national recognition. His book was absorbing, inspirational, personal, but the story it told was a sad one. Still oh, such bright hope shone through the tragedy that the book chronicled. It left my heart about to burst with the joy of it.

Impetuously, I wrote the author, not daring to hope that I'd hear from him in return but, for some reason, waiting and feeling that he might respond. He did. And the thoughts expressed in his correspondence carried all the magic and inspiration of his book. We eventually met for an afternoon conversation. Never again have I experienced moments that had the shape and effect of those spent with him. Afterward, I realized that the afternoon—and the book that inspired it—had been a very special gift to me from God.

In the bright sunshine of a newborn day, in the fresh gentle rain, or in the stark coldness of the earth swept clean with snow, there is evidence of His love. Into each evening, we bring from our day that for which we can be thankful: a warm fire, a new friend, a plot of earth, a good book, and time, for a while, to read.

There have been many times when God has looked at me and told me not to weep and, in His great compassion, brought roses out of the sadness of my life. He has touched the pain, and the bitter tears that covered my cheeks have turned sweet in the recognition of His presence. There have been moments, such as those spent with my author-friend, when God has allowed me to see beyond the veil which often hides His face. In the radiant joy of his presence, I've known that, no matter what life would hold, He would be with me and that there would be fresh flowers and new sunrises for each day.

SPIRITUAL PREP: Psalm 16:11; Isaiah 52:9; Habakkuk 3:18–19; Romans 15:13; 1 Peter 1:8

I Am a Child of God!

Describe a specific time when you were very sad, and God gave you unexpected joy:

PRAYER: Father, help me to recognize the flowers and the bright new sunrises
that You bring into my day. Lift my spirit in praise for the roses You place in my heart.

Exercise 3

· · · · · · · · · · · · · · · ·

A TRIBUTE

Be careful that you do not forget the LORD,
who brought you out of Egypt, out of the land of slavery.
Deuteronomy 6:12

Remind me of Your presence, Father, as I go on with my life. You're the source of all good things in it. Without You, there would be no purpose in ministry, no reason to offer hope to others. You brought me out of slavery. You salvaged my soul and grasped me by the hands to pull me out of the quagmire of despair.

It was You Who created the circumstances in which all that is good in me could reach for a breath of sunlight and win the struggle to survive and bear fruit. Life is good now, full of bright possibilities and exciting opportunities. Lord, let me not forget that it was You Who brought me to this place. It was You Who drew me closer to your breast and gently shaped my life so that it could bear flowers instead of thorns. Let these flowers now be a tribute to Your love and Your patience and Your prudent pruning of my life.

Experience has taught me only too keenly, Lord, that success, even in doing Your work, can tempt me to forget you. I confess that in moments when I'm most aware of the fruits of my labor, I take my eyes off of You and open my life to all sorts of unkind thoughts and jealous ambitions. Not so, at this moment, Lord. I long only to walk the path of life with You.

Take away from me any sinful thoughts and purify my soul. Free my heart from attachment to old ways and from guilt over past wrongs now forgiven. Set my mind on You and let all that I do spring from Your abiding love in my heart. Strengthen my faith until there is no longer room for doubt. Keep ever close so that when I wake in the morning, I'm aware of Your presence and when I retire at night, I do so knowing that we have walked this day together.

SPIRITUAL PREP: Deuteronomy 8:2; 1 Chronicles 16:12; Psalms 77:11–12; 103:1–5; Lamentations 3:21–23

I Am a Child of God!

Now, find a photograph of yourself as an adult. If there is room on the inside front cover of this workbook, place it beneath the photo of you as a child; if there isn't room, attach it to the inside of the back cover. As you go through the next twenty-four hours, allow God to remind you of your value to Him. Look for ways that God touches your heart and then record them here before you go to bed.

Write your own tribute to God:

PRAYER: My Lord and Father, I lift up to You my tribute.

Exercise 4

· · · · · · · · · · · · · · · ·

A SONG OF JOY

The LORD is my strength and my defense; he has become my salvation.
He is my God, and I will praise him, my father's God, and I will exalt him.

Exodus 15:2

Lord, let this be a song of praise
 for being a constant Friend,
 for cleansing me from all my sin,
     for patience with me through all my days,
                 and healing me of errant ways,
     for giving me a new life, touched by the Son;
     for making my world, in all of its confusing reality, a joyful one.

You've blessed my life with purpose, filled it with love,
     guided me in peace with the presence of Your Dove.

Father, let this be a song of praise for all the times You've lifted me up to Your high place, and rested me there in gentle and perfect grace.

SPIRITUAL PREP: Psalms 69:30; 95:1–3; 106:1–2; Revelation 7:12

I Am a Child of God!

Write a song of joy to the Lord for being His child, His beloved. Repeat or sing it as you study the adult photograph of yourself which you placed in this book.

PRAYER: Regardless of what life brings, Lord Jesus, keep Your love and Your praise always in my heart.

Leading a "Free to Be Me" Small Group

Your role as small-group leader is to facilitate personal and spiritual growth in each member. It's not the intent of this book—or of your role as leader—to teach facts, theories, or ways of doing. What you *are* responsible for, as group leader, is to

1. Exercise patience, so that each session unfolds in a way that best helps group members.

2. Trust in the Holy Spirit to guide the members to see and hear that which best meets their needs—and to accept that each member may encounter the Holy Spirit in different ways.

3. Listen.

4. Allow occasional silences. Give the rest of the group opportunities to process what they've heard.

5. Affirm God's guidance and ways in which He speaks to each participant.

In other words: No lecturing, controlling, or "fixing." Your "fix" or solution may not be God's solution for that person.

Group Leader Preparation

1. Spiritually: Always seek God's guidance as a group leader, and remain open to the Holy Spirit's guidance. Pray for each group member and for your journey together.

2. Materially: You'll need . . .

   - a confidential space in which to meet
   - chairs
   - desks or other writing surfaces
   - group ground rules (see General Guidelines below) on flip chart or paper copies
   - Bibles
   - pens and/or pencils; "Free to be Me" workbooks for each member
   - a prayer-request notebook
   - songs and musical accompaniment of some kind, if you wish to include singing

Ideally, you'll want to find a meeting area where confidentiality can be assured. Also, set up your chairs or desks in a circle or square, to encourage interaction between group members. At the same time, allow enough distance between individuals so that they have confidentiality while writing in their journals.

General Guidelines

1. **Decide on a timeframe.** You'll need one and a half to two hours to be set aside for each session. Less is not enough time to warm up, and more time than this creates stress and fatigue.

2. **Confidentiality.** What's said in the group stays in the group. Do not discuss what's shared with others outside the group.

3. **Freedom of Participation.** Opportunities for each member to verbally respond to each question should be encouraged, but not demanded. Any individual has the freedom to "pass" on responding verbally to any of the questions in the workbook.

4. **Form of Participation.** Each member of the group needs to speak in first person ("I," "me," "my," "myself") only and not in second ("you") or third person ("they," "them").

5. **Support—don't "fix."** Discourage judging, "fixing," and dominating the group by any participant. Do not allow interrupting, mocking, belittling, nor cross-talk (conversation between two people, excluding all others).

Again, these are basic rules and guidelines, but some form of these should be a part of your group's DNA. Adjust and adapt them as needed to fit your group's needs.

Now you're ready to have your group time. With that, here's a general format for how to lead your group, followed by some more specific recommendations for your opening and closing sessions. The below assumes that you're working within the hour-and-a-half to two-hour format. Again, adapt these to the needs of your group:

Typical Meeting Agenda:

1. (Approximately one hour) Discuss one journaling question at a time, allowing participants to volunteer or "pass" on sharing their responses. Encourage feedback and sharing following each response. Remember to monitor the discussion and hold it to the following guidelines:
   - Each member of the group speaks in first person ("I," "me," "my," "myself") only, not in second ("you") or third person ("they," "them").
   - Discourage judging, "fixing," and dominating the group by any participant. Do not allow interrupting, mocking, belittling, nor cross-talk (conversation between two people, excluding all others).
2. (Approximately 15 minutes) Ask for prayer requests, and record them in your notebook. Allow volunteer prayer for these requests from group members.
3. Close, if you would like, with a song (group singing, CD, or instrumental)

Week One

> Then you will know the truth, and the truth will set you free.
> John 8:32

1. Write out and display the above verse (John 8:32) on a banner, poster, or flipchart.
2. Welcome each member as he or she arrives.
3. Open in prayer.
4. Begin by saying something like: "This meeting is preparation for a journey together in personal and spiritual growth. Tonight we'll spend time getting to know each other a little better and discussing the guidelines and expectations for the group."
5. Have each member introduce himself/herself by sharing:
   a. his/her name
   b. if they're in school, college, or where they work, and telling about their major or job
   c. their favorite pastime
   d. current family (including pets)
6. Restate that the purpose of the group is to work toward personal and spiritual growth as they share experiences, affirmations, and hope with each other. Encourage group members to claim John 8:23 as they work through the book and engage in the journaling. Also encourage them in the knowledge that God can free them from any hurts and hang-ups and give them a new freedom to experience His joy, His peace, and His love.

7. Hand out *Free to Be Me* books to everyone, and go over the content with the group so that each member will understand the process of reading, "Spiritual prep," journaling, discussion, and prayer that will frame each session together. Emphasize the the journaling for each exercise is to be completed prior to coming to the group meeting.

8. Discuss materials needed. (See the **"Group Leader Preparation" section above if needed.)** Ask participants to bring Bibles, workbook, pencils, and open minds to each meeting.

9. Ask participants to complete the journaling parts, "Getting to Know Myself as a Child of God" and "Living as a Child of God" of Exercise 1 in Step 1 before your next meeting. Let your group members know that this will be the pattern going forward; each exercise will be completed at home prior to discussing that particular exercise in the group meeting.

10. Go over the group rules together. (Again, consult the General Guidelines section above as needed.) Make sure everyone understands and agrees with your group rules before moving on.

11. Brainstorm: Ask the following questions one at a time, and give time to record all responses on a flip-chart or blackboard:

    a. What are your hopes and expectations for the time ahead of us in this group?

    b. What are your anxieties about this time together?

12. Focus: Read the author's introduction to the workbook.

13. Remind participants to complete the journaling portions of Step 1, Exercise 1 before the next meeting.

14. Start your "prayer-request" list. Say something like, "Prayer requests will be recorded by the leader. Each week we will spend some time as a group praying for the requests. Confidentiality applies here also. What is said in the group stays in the group, including the prayer requests."

15. Close your initial session in prayer, committing your hopes and fears from the brainstorming session to God. Also prayer for any requests mentioned.

Week Two: Step 1, Exercise 1: Out from Behind the Mask
· ·

Note: Because each session will follow the same basic agenda—with any modifications that you, as leader, feel are needed—this agenda will be outlined only once for this first exercise.

1. Welcome group members, and open with prayer.

2. Leader reads aloud to the group the introductory story, in this case: Anna's story.

3. Read the opening Scripture verse: 1 Samuel 16:7

4. Spiritual Prep: Again, take one verse at a time. Let a group member read each verse, then take a little time as a group to react to it and how it pertains to this week's topic. For example:

    a. Psalm 51:6: God's desire for us involves what sort of truth?

    b. John 7:24: This verse tells us not to judge by appearance, but according to "righteous judgment": What do you think the writer means by "righteous judgment?"

5. Ask if each person has completed the journaling section of Exercise One, "Getting to Know Myself as a

Child of God" and "Living as a Child of God." If not, you may want to allow 15–20 minutes for them to do so, but stress verbally that the journaling section should be completed before coming to the meeting.

6. Discuss each journal question one at a time. Go around the group, allowing each participant to either answer or "pass." Allow gentle questions and affirmative discussion as each participant shares his or her answer to each of the thought questions (not needed for the single-answer fact questions).

7. Once you're done with your journal discussion, allow a few more minutes afterward for general discussion of the topic.

8. Take prayer requests. As participants make requests, be sure to write them in your prayer notebook.

9. Close your group time in prayer and—and if you'd like, by singing and/or playing a worship song (on CD).

Weeks 3–51:

Continue to follow the above agenda, with modifications as you feel are needed or led to make.

Week 52: Closure

1. Before your group time:
    - Prepare a double-spaced list of every participant in the group. Make enough copies of the list for each participant.
    - Also, bring several pairs of scissors to the meeting—enough for every two or three members to share a set. Set them up around your circle/square before your meeting time.
    - You'll also need one small bottle of glue.
    - Celebration Option: You may also wish to offer some sort of small certificate to each person who completes the program. This can be done in a very relaxed way or in a more formal setting followed by a finger-food celebration.

2. Open with greeting and a prayer.

3. Do the following affirmation exercise together:
    a. Distribute a copy of the lists you prepared to each member of the group. Allow enough silent time for each member to write something they've come to like and/or admire about each person on the list.
    b. As people complete their lists of affirmations, have them cut the affirmations, each paired with the correct name, into strips—and have them hang on to their comments after cutting them into strips.
    c. Put one chair in the center of the circle—your "hot seat"—and put your bottle of glue next to it.
    d. Have one person at a time take the "hot seat." Give the person in the hot seat a bottle of glue, and have them open their workbooks to the last, blank page in the book.
    e. While the individual remains in the hot seat, each member of the group will read his/her affirmation of that person, and then give their strips of to the person in the hot seat. Give the person in the hot seat time to glue each strip of paper on his/her blank workbook page.

f. Go on to the next group member, and repeat the process until everyone's had a chance to sit in the hot seat and glue their strips of paper to their workbooks.

3. If you're doing the Celebration Option, present your certificates now, to further your celebration of each group member's accomplishment and contribution to the group. Allow time during or after your celebration for individual group members to share feedback on how helpful the program has been, how they feel about their own progress since beginning the program, and what improvements they'd like to see made to the program.

4, Close your time in prayer, thanking God for everything He's done through your group members, and for everything He has yet do in their lives as they further become *Free to Be Me*.